peopleScapes
PUBLISHING

Produced and published in the United States of America by PeopleScapes Inc.
Printed in the Republic of Korea by Doosan Printing.

First Edition

Library of Congress Cataloging in Publication Control Number: 2002111244

ISBN 0-9673485-4-4

PREVIOUS PAGE: Fishermen pause on the Missouri River's glassy surface during a foggy July morning east of Yankton. Below Gavins Point Dam, the Missouri returns to its treacherous, beautiful self until it becomes channelized at Ponca State Park in Nebraska.

The

MISSOURI

South Dakota's River Legend

Photographs by GREG LATZA *Text by* KEVIN WOSTER

Design and Editing by JODI HOLLEY LATZA

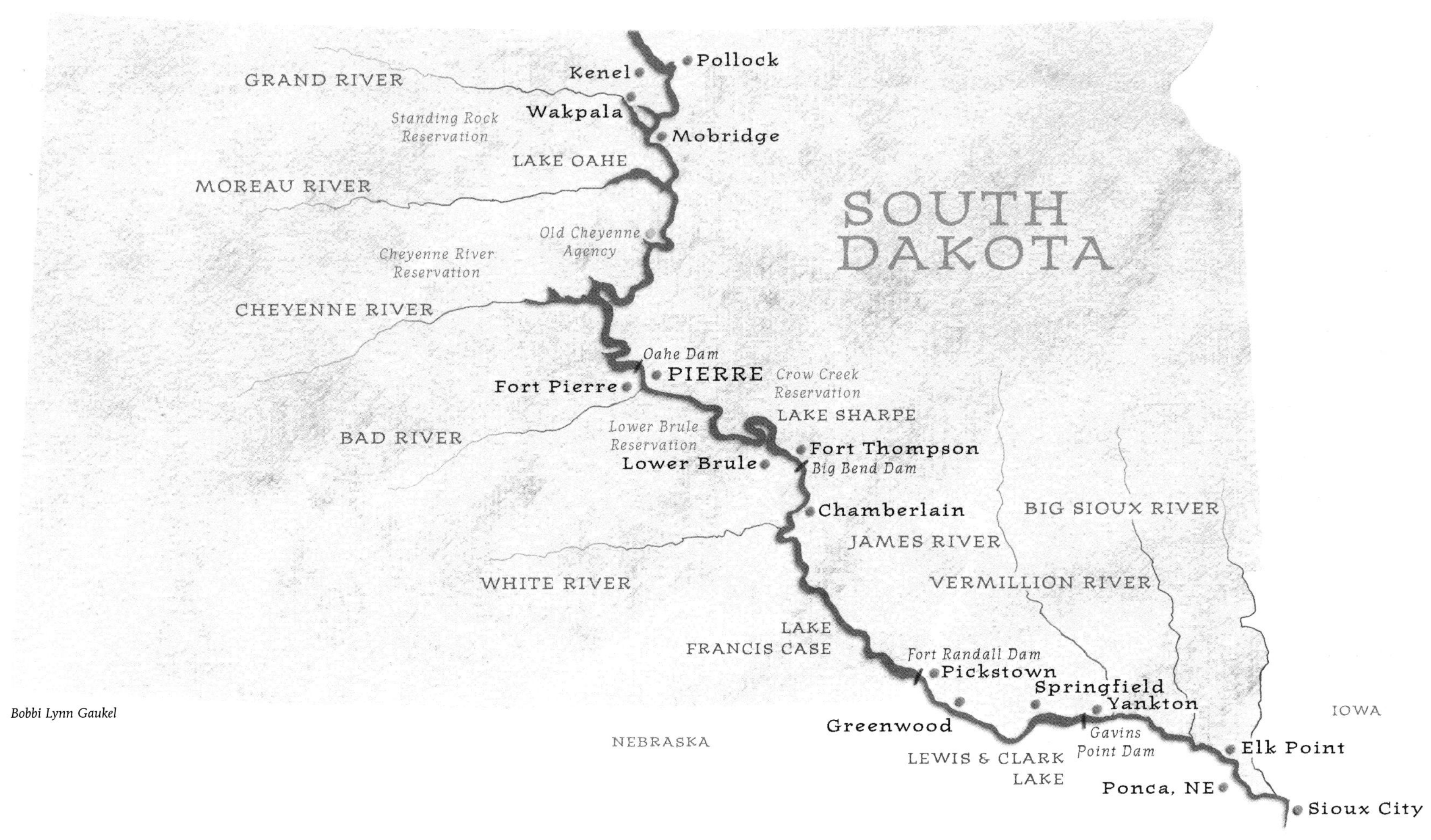

Bobbi Lynn Gaukel

Lazy Giant

14

Northern Border
to
Old Cheyenne Agency

of Wisdom and Power

42

Old Cheyenne Agency
to
Pierre

Teaching Tolerance

70

Pierre
to
Chamberlain

Creating Opportunity

108

Chamberlain
to
Springfield

Inspiring Survival

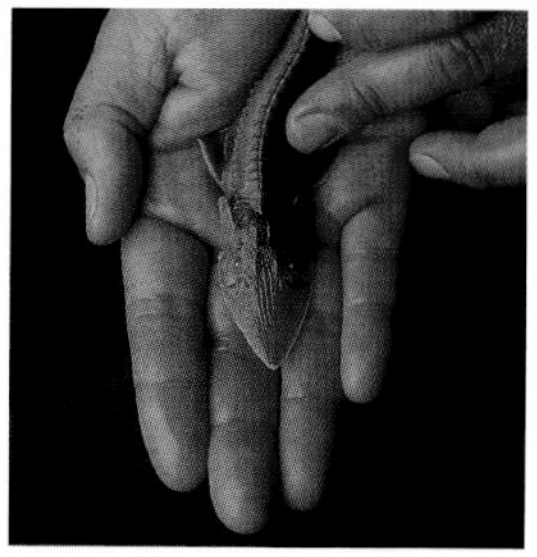

138

Springfield
to
Sioux City

Foreword 7

Acknowledgements 170

Production Notes 171

Index 172

The Missouri River passes eastward beneath Yankton's Meridian Bridge. Completed in 1924, the bridge helped to complete the International Meridian Highway, now known as Highway 81, which still routes motorists between Mexico and Canada. Having served as the capital of Dakota Territory from 1861 to 1883, Yankton remains an integral part of Missouri River history.

An Ageless and Watery Road

By BERNIE HUNHOFF

We were flying in a small plane from Yankton to Pierre on a cave-black night. Our only guide lights were courtesy of farms and towns several thousand feet below us.

The pilot knew the plane; I knew South Dakota, at least in daylight on the ground. We thought we might have flown too far west. Not being accustomed to the dark and eerie aerial view of a state I'd traveled extensively, I couldn't be sure.

We joked about staying overnight in Rapid City if we ran into mountains. We were about to turn back east when we found the Missouri, easily visible as a north-south strip of total darkness, uninterrupted by yard lights or street lamps. With the river as our guide, in less than an hour we landed at the Pierre Municipal Airport.

What a path the Missouri cuts across South Dakota.

John Milton, the late professor of English at the University of South Dakota, liked to refer to the Missouri as The Big Road because, before the dams, it was a thoroughfare for travelers. That night it was a road for us to follow.

But the Missouri means more to us than any hard road. Its economic, military, agricultural, environmental, sporting and cultural implications have endured as long as man has lived here. Flowing through seven states, the 2,341-mile Missouri is the world's eighth longest river. It would rank third if we could persuade mapmakers that the Mississippi is just its tributary.

But better bragging rights would not change the Missouri. The river is bigger than hard facts. It is part of America's collective soul, as you'll discover in *The Missouri: South Dakota's River Legend.* Greg Latza's photographs and Kevin Woster's essays remind me of the people we've met and the stories we've encountered at *South Dakota Magazine* since we began publication in 1985. They also harken to my childhood.

My brothers and I all were born at Yankton's Sacred Heart Hospital, which sits on a chalkstone bluff above the river. We did a little fishing, not much, in its waters. But we swam in its murky water, romanced girls on the rocky shores, found summer jobs with the Corps of Engineers, and proudly took visiting relatives past the massive Gavins Point Dam power plant and the huge gates that gush foam when the Corps reduces Lewis and Clark Lake and raises the river. An eccentric great-uncle occasionally came from northern South Dakota to fish in the lake. He caught catfish so big that they looked like passengers in the backseat of his old Ford.

Married with two kids of my own, we camped under the big cottonwoods by the lake. Every summer, we rejoined my brothers for outings by Fort Randall, an hour's drive west. We also had a family reunion upriver on Lake Oahe near Mobridge. The river is the river, no matter what stretch you're on at the time. It feels the same whether I'm in Chamberlain or Omaha or St. Louis. Call it camaraderie among river rats.

On one particular Fourth of July, our family was picnicking by Lewis and Clark Lake when a young woman asked us to help find her missing boy. She was calmly recruiting everyone. Some people searched up and down the shore. Some combed the beach and the adjacent groves of trees. Some walked through waist-deep water, hoping they would bump into nothing softer than a rock or a beer bottle.

There was no panic. Surely, the boy would show up — sleeping in the backseat of a stranger's car or chasing butterflies in the trees. All was calm. Then a young man's foot bumped into the boy under the water. The man cradled the boy like a baby and carried him to the sand. A nurse in a bathing suit gave him mouth-to-mouth. Medics arrived. They left with the boy. His obituary was in the next day's paper. It all happened quietly, with the sound of the waves loudly licking at the rocks.

We love the Missouri, but the Missouri is indifferent about us. It makes itself felt to people who come near. It changes lives, usually as slowly as it washes at a chalkstone bluff; other times, change floods in faster than can be comprehended by the human mind. Despite our unequal relationship, the river becomes part of our soul.

The river has always been rich with drama. Buffalo roamed its banks in herds so huge they turned the banks brown as far as the eye could see, according to early explorers. In winter, they crossed the river on the ice. At times, their cumulative weight was too much and whole herds fell into the icy water and died. When the river level is low, a skull or bone sometimes surfaces in the sand.

Also buried in the river near Yankton is a steamboat called the *Western*. It was sunk by an ice jam and flood in March of 1881. Like the buffalo skulls, the *Western* sometimes reveals its skeleton in low water. Altogether, about 30 such ships are buried between Yankton and Omaha. They were not

Woolly verbana blooms above the clover-covered breaks near the White River mouth in Lyman County. Considered a nuisance by ranchers, the plant was utilized by the Lakota to make an effective stomachache remedy.

Thick, heaving ice below Fort Randall Dam offers winter sport for ice fishermen. As the third of four main-stem dams along the Missouri River in South Dakota, Fort Randall Dam contains 107-mile long Lake Francis Case.

primitive, over-sized rafts but finely built ships that measured over 200 feet in length and carried hundreds of tons of cargo to Dakota Territory. If you believe local legend, the *North Alabama*, which went down near Vermillion, was carrying treasure of some sort.

Before Gavins Point Dam created Lewis and Clark Lake, Yankton was known as the city that hung Jack McCall in 1877, lost the territorial capital in 1883 and replaced it with an institution for the mentally ill. The lake was a badly needed bump. It started a tourism industry in a river valley previously inhabited by ranchers, cows and those big catfish. Houses were built in the hills north of the lake. The state built a marina. Boats, some as big as small ships, dropped anchor. Restaurants, shops and bait stops sprouted along Highway 52.

About 50 river miles from Yankton, in the extreme southeast corner of South Dakota, the river – and South Dakota's friendly tax climate – attracted the creators of Dakota Dunes, one of America's most affluent and newest communities. The new city makes Union County one of the nine wealthiest in the United States. Million dollar homes and some of the Midwest's best-known corporations have been built on the sandy riverside soil.

Going upstream, however, economic benefits of the river – pre- or post-dam – are less apparent. Though a tourism industry exists, it hasn't spread Dunes-style prosperity. In fact, some of America's poorest families live along and near the river valley on the Crow Creek, Lower Brule, Standing Rock and Cheyenne Indian reservations.

Golf courses, hunting lodges, residential developments and other amenities are taking root in the expansive landscape along the Missouri. In some cases, tribal officials are initiating the development. In other places, white ranchers and farmers are looking for ways to supplement their income. Examples of both can be found in this book, like the farming operations developed by the Crow Creek and Lower Brule tribes and Lee and Trudy Qualm, who started a hunting lodge on their Platte farm.

Hilly, rocky land within a rifle shot of the Missouri often brings a better price than the best Lincoln County corn ground. Yet, the men and women who run cattle on that same land or use it to grow wheat are being squeezed by the whims of Mother Nature and a world economy that seldom rewards raw production, even when the product is food.

Despite its generally placid surface, the Missouri has been a valley of controversy and adventure ever since Meriwether Lewis and William Clark journeyed this way in 1804. The people and places you'll meet on the following pages represent our river culture. Greg Latza and Kevin Woster are sons of the state. South Dakotans are fortunate that the two have been able to earn a living with their creative talents without emigrating like so many of their contemporaries. Their photos and prose remind me both of what the river was like before our time, and how today's society is shaped by the ageless and watery road.

The small town mayors, family farmers, tribal leaders, sportsmen and historians featured by Latza and Woster provide human drama to the river valley. Altwin Grassrope comes from a long line of Lower Brule leaders. Springfield Mayor Norm Schelske, a happy-go-lucky saloonkeeper by trade, has been fighting to fix the sediment problem on Lewis and Clark Lake for years. Bob Hipple was a legend in South Dakota newspapering; he loved the river and his native state with passion, and with humility. When the state's press association honored Hipple a few years before his death, he modestly shrugged it off, saying he just happened to hang around long enough to be noticed.

The same might be humbly said of the Missouri. As the years pass, we gain a better appreciation for its importance in South Dakota. Meanwhile, the river is indifferent. It acts as if it knows it will outlast us all.

Bernie Hunhoff is a fifth-generation South Dakotan who worked in newspapering and politics before founding South Dakota Magazine *in 1985. He has been publisher and editor of the magazine ever since. He and his staff of 10 publish from an old territorial governor's house in downtown Yankton, just two blocks from the Missouri River.*

Boats leave trails of light on Lewis and Clark Lake as a family watches television in their shore-bound camper. Although it's summer, strings of Christmas lights offer ground illumination for nighttime activity. Nearly 2 million outdoor enthusiasts visit Lewis and Clark Lake each year, participating in fishing, hiking, sailing, swimming, archery, biking, birdwatching, diving and other outdoor activities.

Lazy Giant ...

When the Missouri River enters South Dakota today, it is a very different river than the "Big Muddy" or "Mighty Mo" that lives in legend and inspires poetry and song.

It is a lake, not a river, really. Wide and flat and open to the prairie winds, it moves imperceptibly as it crosses the boundary from North Dakota to South, as if sneaking in unannounced.

It is nothing at all like the river Meriwether Lewis and William Clark relied on 200 years ago, when they challenged an unknown frontier by lugging and prodding and rowing rough-hewn wooden crafts against the muscular current.

It was a crafty, fickle snake of a river then, changing course on a whim, rearing up to ravage the surrounding landscape in the spring and settling down to quiet, brown somnolence by late summer and fall.

It was a river of paddlefish and sturgeon, catfish and gar, with shorelines busy with terns and plovers and upland dotted with buffalo and elk.

It was a river of bounty, of hardship, of unimaginable potential.

The North Dakota-South Dakota border stretches across a bulging Missouri River a few miles north of Kenel.

It is something quite different today. It is shaped and controlled – if not entirely tamed – by six massive hydroelectric dams, four of which are in South Dakota. The Missouri as we know it here is largely a string of reservoirs, connected by fleeting vestiges of the old river self: water pours from dams and tugs and pulls at clay banks and cottonwood roots on its way to the next controlled pool.

Two semi-natural stretches in southeast South Dakota are wild enough to be designated as national recreational rivers. But most of the Missouri here is water best known for its walleye, and the $40 million generated each year by the sport fishing industry.

It is a place of riverside irrigation, municipal and rural water supplies and phenomenal power generation. The dams help provide downstream flood control and water sufficient to float barges that carry commodities from Sioux City, Iowa, to St. Louis, Missouri.

The buffalo and elk are gone from its bluffs. And the dams, for all the good they brought, have left a legacy of loss, in endangered species, siltation, streamside erosion and conflict with tribal people who unwillingly sacrificed much of their culture and some of their villages to the reservoirs.

Yet the old, calm river still wields power as it moves through the reservoirs it shapes and emerges as itself below the dams. Lanniko Lee, a tribal teacher and writer who saw her family land swallowed by massive Lake Oahe, still believes in the power of the river.

"It's still there, if we stop and feel it," she says. "The river wisdom is there, if we pay attention. It has the power to instruct, and the power to heal."

All through river country people who believe in river wisdom have discovered a balance between the old river and the new, yesterday's Missouri and today's. The river can forge connections that transcend time and race. Jack Shillingstad, his wife Teresa and the young American Indian students at the Wakpala school prove that every day.

Shillingstad is a rancher and school principal, his wife a horsewoman. Together, in the landscape along Oak Creek in the Missouri River breaks, they run a horsemanship program that connects young tribal members with their past.

It's learning to ride, and a lot more. It leads to traditional dance, song and hand-made clothing, and to horseback camping trips to traditional campsites along the river. It leads some to make the 300-mile horseback pilgrimage from the camp of Sitting Bull not far from Wakpala to the Wounded Knee memorial gravesite on the Pine Ridge Reservation.

The Big Foot Ride honors the 1890 journey of Chief Big Foot and his people, memorializing the tragic massacre of so many of them at the hands of U.S. soldiers.

"The kids soak this stuff up like sponges," Shillingstad says. "They're learning about their ancestors, their past, the way life was along this river long ago."

They're learning about themselves, too. The river can teach you that – as Lanniko Lee says – if you give it a chance.

RIGHT: A simple quartzite post marks the border between North Dakota and South Dakota, just east of the Missouri River. In 1889, the federal government appropriated $25,000 for the task of identifying the newly formed border. As a result, markers were placed every half mile – 720 in all – stretching from Minnesota to Montana.

FOLLOWING PAGES: Cattle graze peacefully among the rolling hills and autumn colors south of Pollock.

S.D.

Elaine St. John never heard the woman speak, but she heard the stories from those who did.

It was the voice of a woman, a mournful moan reaching into a wail, calling up from the Missouri River shoreline to find the ears of tribal people on the Standing Rock Indian Reservation near the small town of Kenel.

It was a voice in misery, a voice searching for a way home.

"We believe it was her, and that it was coming from down there where we believe old Fort Manuel was," St. John says, stepping easily through crumbling shale and shining stones along the west shore of the Missouri, then stopping to point to the dense willow stands a quarter mile away. "Down in there somewhere is where she lived – and where she was buried – the Bird Woman. People used to hear her crying."

The woman of this local legend is believed to have been Sacagawea, the Shoshone girl who accompanied explorers Meriwether Lewis, William Clark and their Corps of Discovery up the Missouri River and on to the Pacific Ocean in 1804. She had been captured by the Hidatsa tribe, taken from her homeland in what is now Idaho and sold to a French trader who accompanied Lewis and Clark.

By most accounts, Sacagawea, also called Bird Woman, returned to the Fort Manuel area in northern South Dakota after the expedition. She lived there for a few years before she took ill and died. Her spirit lived on in folklore and, to those who heard the voice, in fact.

Then one summer a group of Shoshone people came to Kenel to help the Bird Woman's spirit find its way home. St. John took the group down by the river, where Fort Manuel is believed to have stood. There they performed a Shoshone ceremony to free the spirit of Bird Woman.

"It was close to evening, and the water was still," St. John says. "And while they were performing the ceremony a bunch of small white birds flew behind us, above the water, and they were talking, like they were consenting to what we were doing. Then a flock of bigger birds came and flew right above us. And then her spirit was lifted. She is no longer there.

"At least, that's what I believe."

St. John, 72, is a devout Catholic who has no trouble blending her tribal spirituality with her more traditional Christian faith. She sees signs of a mysterious power in the birds and other wildlife of the Missouri River breaks as surely as she does in the

Elaine St. John holds a Lakota hymnal she used for worship at the original site of the Assumption of the Blessed Virgin Mary Catholic Church in old Kenel. The town was moved to a high hill above this Missouri River flat in the late 1950s to prepare for the creation of Lake Oahe.

services at the Assumption of the Blessed Virgin Mary Catholic Church in Kenel, where she attends Mass.

The Rev. Steve Biegler has no problem with that mixture in spiritual beliefs.

"You see that often," Biegler says. "People here refer to eagles, for example, as a significant sign. They always look for them when we are burying someone, and often they will see one, if not at the burial, during the days of mourning. And owls, of course, can be seen as a sign of death."

There was a time when the Catholic church tried to discourage tribal people from believing in such spiritual symbols. But Biegler says the church is learning from tribal people, as is he. Now, a more enlightened church respects and even reveres cultural beliefs that do not conflict with the Gospel, he says.

He sees no conflict in the image of eagles and owls and speeding shorebirds as being of God. Growing up on a ranch near Timber Lake, Biegler, 43, understands the value his congregation places in wildlife and wild places. When the Assumption of the Blessed Virgin Mary church was rebuilt after a fire in 2000, it included an altar made from a mammoth cottonwood – a tree that symbolizes strength and endurance to people in river country.

It's also the tree where eagles nest, and that has profound meaning to many in Biegler's congregation.

"God speaks to us in ways we can relate to, in ways people can understand," he says. "The people here understand those symbols. They're open to them. And I really believe that in moments I've been there with them, it wasn't just happenstance that an eagle or other bird flew over. I think God is using symbols to console them at that time."

Or, as with the spirit of Sacagawea, to console them many years later.

Monsignor William O'Connell greets parishioners at the Assumption of the Blessed Virgin Mary Catholic Church in Kenel. The church has a long history of survival. First built in 1880, the church originally known as St. Benedict's was destroyed by a tornado. The next church built on the same site in 1930 was named the Assumption of the Blessed Virgin Mary Church. That structure escaped flood when it was moved with the rest of Kenel to avoid rising Lake Oahe, then burned down in 1971. The church was rebuilt, only to succumb to a lightning strike and subsequent fire in 1998. Rebuilt once again, it now boasts an altar made from a huge cottonwood tree, a symbol of strength and endurance to its Lakota congregation.

LEFT: Springtime prairie grasses cover rangeland along the eastern border of Standing Rock Indian Reservation where the Kline Buttes rise to meet the sky.

RIGHT: Sylvan Beautiful Bald Eagle, a traditional dancer from Wakpala, ties on his feathers prior to the 9th Annual Kenel Wacipi. "It's been two years since I danced," he said. "This is a great place to start again."

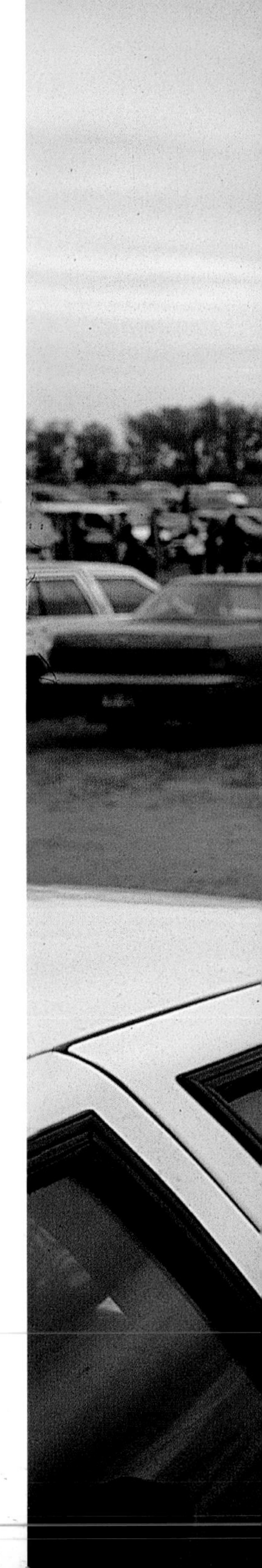

Gordy Atkinson motors over the site of his boyhood home, now submerged beneath Lake Oahe.

Bobbing along in his old fiberglass tri-hull on Lake Oahe, Gordy Atkinson can see two views of the Missouri River: One is the choppy, blue-green lake that stretches for miles into a sultry summer afternoon. The other is the river that flows forever in his memory.

He's not sure which he likes best.

"There were good things about both, you know," says Atkinson, 72, a retired meat cutter and grocery store owner from Pollock. "I like what this lake gives us a lot – the boating and the walleye fishing and the tourism. And, of course, we don't have the flooding like we used to. That's a big reason they built the dam."

The dam is Oahe, a 2-mile long, 245-foot high monster of creative engineering, five miles north of Pierre and about 160 miles south of Pollock. It created the mammoth reservoir that covers more than 350,000 surface acres, the reservoir that destroyed the other river that Atkinson remembers so well.

"That old river was nice, too," Atkinson says, slow-motoring his boat along the east shore of Oahe, about 2 miles northwest of Pollock. "We had all those trees and all the wildlife, the sandbars and everything. I don't know, I guess I see good in both of them."

On this day, as Atkinson and his wife, Marilyn, take one of their countless cruises on the big lake, the memories of the past seem as strong as today's reality. Soon Atkinson arrives at his childhood home – a riverside ranch that now rests in concrete remains under the surface of Oahe.

"It was right here," he says, nudging the throttle down a click or two and letting the boat drift with the southeast wind. "The house was over there, and there was a barn and chicken coop. It was part of the old Smith Ranch, which was once the largest alfalfa ranch in the world."

The sprawling operation relied on the rich soils of the river bottom to produce extraordinary alfalfa crops and to supply crucial paid labor for job-hungry men during the difficult 1930s. Atkinson's father, W.H. Atkinson, leased a portion of that ranch, raising Hereford cattle and alfalfa and impressive corn crops – an odd commodity in the otherwise parched central South Dakota ranch country.

"Oh yeah, corn grew well down on that river bottom," Atkinson says. "It was a nice place."

But it was destined, along with thousands of acres of river bottom ground, to be lost to the new reality of the Missouri. By the time Atkinson was in high school, his dad had given up on the ranch, moved his family to what is now called Old Pollock, and was running a meat market. When Gordy graduated from high school in 1948, he joined his father in that business, and he and Marilyn settled into a rented home in town and started their family.

By the early 1950s, however, Oahe Dam already was taking shape. And by the late 1950s, it was taking fields and trees and the remnants of homes all along its lowlands. The entire town of Pollock was flooded after most of the homes and businesses first relocated to higher ground nearby.

The federal government bought each structure, then gave the owner a chance to buy it back at "salvage" price. Most did.

"We moved about everything, except those buildings — like the brick ones — you couldn't move. They knocked those down so they wouldn't be a hazard," Atkinson says. "There were days when five or six houses would be going up the hill. You'd look out the window and see a house going down Main Street."

Atkinson moved his house, then watched the rising waters of Oahe flood the foundation and sidewalks. After the lake filled, he and others would take boats over the town, looking down on clear days to see the remains of their former homes. And when the water in the reservoir fell to record lows in the late 1980s, Old Pollock emerged again and people returned to kick the foundations of their past.

"The sidewalks were still there, and the streets. And you could just walk to your old house and look at the footing," Atkinson says. "It sure gave you a funny feeling."

Gulls rest on a sandbar at Old Pollock. Once an ordinary prairie town, the site is now covered by Pollock Bay and adjacent Lake Pocasse, its streets occupied by pike and walleye instead of cars, trucks and pedestrians.

LEFT: Saint Elizabeth's Mission soaks up a fiery prairie sunset on the banks of Oak Creek near Wakpala. Chief Gall, a leader during the Battle of Little Bighorn, donated land for the church and is buried in St. Elizabeth's cemetery. Masses today are celebrated in both English and Lakota.

RIGHT: Erosion claims a grass-covered bank near Gallaway Bay, dusting driftwood with sand and gravel and exposing years of sedimentation. During high water years, one windy day can carve several inches from such fragile banks.

LEFT: Bobbi Three Legs rides Cisco through the underbrush bordering Oak Creek behind the Wakpala Public School.

RIGHT: Ajay Fox grooms a pony as Kolt Tiger awaits his turn to ride. Students in the Wakpala Horse Program learn horsemanship under the direction of Jack Shillingstad, school principal and local rancher. "The kids soak this stuff up like sponges," Shillingstad says. "They're learning about their ancestors, their past, the way life was along this river long ago."

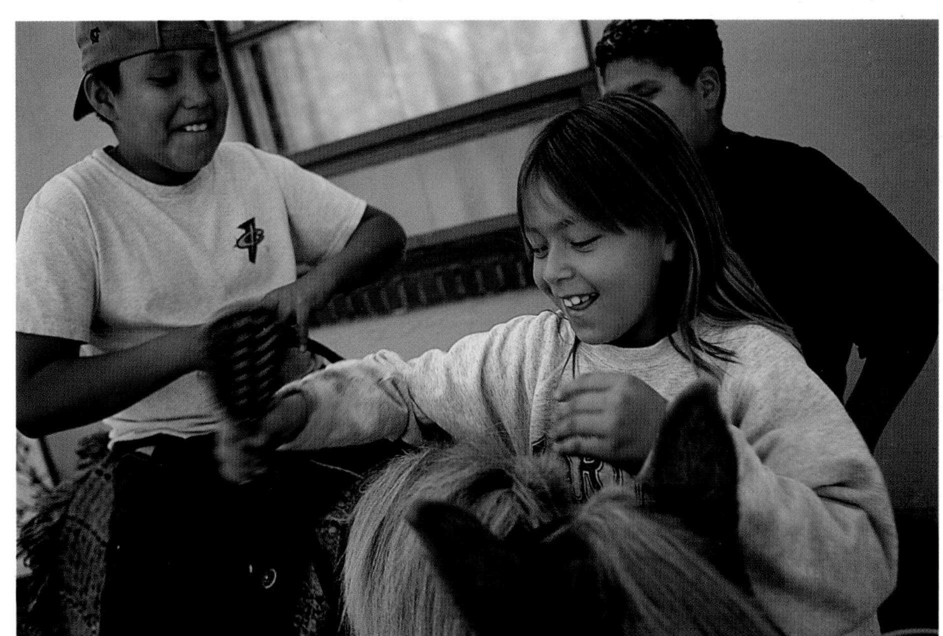

Like most of his friends and neighbors, Jim Schott enjoys a mild autumn day hunting sharp-tailed grouse in the rugged river breaks east of his ranch.

But his favorite kind of hunting adds an element of human danger that an upland bird like the grouse just can't provide.

"None of it compares with rattlesnake hunting," says the 58-year-old cattle rancher from McLaughlin. "If I had my choice to go bird hunting or snake hunting, it would be snake hunting."

Schott has his choice frequently in the fall, living as he does in some of South Dakota's best rattlesnake country. That might seem like a contradiction in terms, since many people see snakes, especially the poisonous prairie rattlesnakes of Missouri River country, as the slithering incarnations of outdoor evil.

That's not at all how Schott sees them.

"I don't hate them," he says. "How can I say it? They're just part of the outdoors. I enjoy them and I respect them."

In their place, of course. And Schott doesn't think their place includes his back step, or garden, or the middle of the yard when he's mowing the lawn. Yet, such was the situation at his ranch many years ago. And it troubled him, because the rattlers that slipped into his ranch headquarters and lay quietly alongside the house were a daily threat to his wife and family during the warm months.

"When we first moved out here in the early 1970s, we'd step out of the house and there'd be snakes. We'd find snakes who knows where around the yard. It just wasn't safe for children."

Schott didn't want to wipe out rattlesnakes on his ranch. He simply felt that something had to be done. And in the 1980s, his father-in-law, Connie Dietrich of Mobridge, provided a beginning.

"He was out on horseback, riding through a large prairie dog town in the fall of the year, and there were just snakes all over," Schott said. "They were in there to den up for the winter, and it was warm and they were out of the holes sunning themselves."

Dietrich began hunting the snakes, waiting for autumn when rattlers that had been scattered across the sweeping pastures of western wheat and green needle grass returned to their winter quarters, where they would survive the cold below the frost line.

The ground outside those dens affords a bounty for snake hunters. And after a while listening to stories of his father-in-law's hunts, Schott joined him. Hunting mostly in prairie dog towns, they used dandelion

An agitated rattlesnake tests the air on the prairie north of Mobridge. The prairie rattlesnake can grow to nearly five feet in length, and it's not uncommon for several hundred to congregate in a single prairie dog colony prior to winter.

pickers, sharpened and modified so they could be poked around in a prairie dog hole to find and drag out a rattler.

The snake-hunting crew later grew to include other family members and friends. On exceptionally productive autumn days, the group sometimes took more than 100 rattlers. Schott believes such success reduced the snake population in and around his ranch to a level that's safer for people and livestock, while still leaving plenty of rattlers on his land.

Schott's father-in-law has since given up the hunt, and now his sons, Jared and Jason, are off working in Washington, D.C. and Minneapolis. And though his wife, Priscilla, has trailed along on past snake hunts, these days, Schott usually goes alone. No longer does he take huge numbers of snakes. Now he's looking for size.

"I'm after a 5-footer. I've come within a couple inches."

Schott doesn't bother rattlers outside of his autumn hunts. And they don't bother him. A while back, out in the river breaks on horseback, he decided to take a break, climb up on a clay knob above the Missouri and enjoy the view.

"I suppose I sat there on the ground for 10 or 20 minutes, and when I got ready to leave there was a rattler all coiled up 2 or 3 feet away," Schott says. "Sometime while I was sitting there, he crawled up and joined me."

The snake never buzzed or acted menacing in any way. And Schott returned the favor, quietly getting up and walking away. He never felt threatened.

"I guess, thinking back," he says, "I'd turn my back on a snake like that before I'd turn it on some people."

Jim Schott empties a newly harvested bucket of rattlesnakes into a larger container as daughter Vickie looks on. A couple of hours of snake hunting produced two dozen rattlers in a massive 900-acre prairie dog colony nestled along the Missouri River east of Wakpala.

LEFT: Saddle bronc riders prepare for their event to begin at the annual Sitting Bull Stampede in Mobridge. Each year, several rodeos are hosted here during the Fourth of July holiday, drawing rodeo talent from across the country. ABOVE: Canine Quazi seems to revel in the limelight as the Oahe Vet Hospital float cruises the Sitting Bull Stampede Parade route through Mobridge.

LEFT: Pebbles find themselves stranded atop pillars of sand after wave action erodes a beach south of Mobridge.

RIGHT: A bust of Sitting Bull, carved by Crazy Horse Monument artist Korczak Ziolkowski, overlooks his gravesite and the western shore of the river south of Mobridge. Area rancher, teacher and sculptor Jack Shillingstad carved an accompanying memorial plaque for the site and has repaired damage to the Sitting Bull bust over the years. "I admire Sitting Bull," he says. "He was noble, wise, honest and a fighter. He was endowed with all the traits we look for and brag about when we want to express what it means to be an American."

1834–1890
SITTING BULL
TATANKA IYOTAKE
Sitting Bull was born on the Grand River a few miles west of Mobridge. His tragic end came at the very place he was born. He was shot when being arrested because of his alleged involvement with the Ghost Dance Craze.
Sitting Bull was originally buried at Fort Yates, ND. On April 8, 1953 surviving relatives with the aid of the Dakota Memorial Association moved his remains to the present location and dedicated the Memorial Burial Site April 11, 1953.
1876 - Victorious at the Battle of Little Big Horn
1877 - Sought asylum in Canada.
1881 - Returned to the United States.
1885 - Toured with Buffalo Bill's Wild West Show

... of Wisdom and Power ...

When Lanniko Lees drifts in a small boat on the waters of Lake Oahe, or stands quietly on its shores, she often sees one thing and feels another.

The Missouri River of her eyes is not the Missouri River of her heart.

Because, she believes, somewhere in that blue-green behemoth of a lake called Oahe, the old river runs as wildly and surely, if not as obviously, as it did before engineers and work crews for the U.S. Army Corps of Engineers tied it up in ropes of earth and concrete.

Dams or not, the river lives.

"You can feel it. There's a power there, an intelligence," says Lee, a teacher, writer and member of the Cheyenne River Sioux Tribe who knew the old river briefly as a child. "It still has the power to instruct, and the power to heal."

Lee learned of that power growing up with her parents and grandparents, siblings and friends, along the west shore of the old Missouri River, west of Gettysburg. They swam in the river, bathed in it, caught catfish and buffalo fish to be fried and smoked, collected wild grapes and plums and chokecherries from its bottomland forest, gathered teas and herbs and hunted deer and rabbit and grouse in its rugged breaks.

The river sustained them, physically and spiritually. And then it was gone, taking with it a way of life for tribal people up and down the Missouri.

When Oahe Dam was built, it displaced thousands of people, Indian and non-Indian. Ranchers took government money and tried to rebuild their cow-calf operations on higher ground, or on land away from the Missouri. Some found other jobs in town, or left the region entirely. And some still search for a new life in commercial guiding or resort operations, or subdividing property for housing.

But no one had to look harder for a new life than tribal people. Oahe took more tribal land than any other dam, flooding more than 150,000 acres on the Cheyenne River and Standing Rock reservations. More than 100,000 acres were lost on Cheyenne River alone, forcing hundreds of people from their homes, and from their old lifestyle.

Gone were homes and fields and gardens and ceremonial sites. And in some instances, Oahe swallowed archaeological treasures and the gravesites of tribal ancestors. Although the remains were supposed to be moved by the Corps, in some cases

Lanniko Lee's turtle-shaped ring is a constant reminder of her childhood on the river. "The turtle is the one creature that knows the depth of the water and fullness of the earth," she explains. "The blues and greens in the stone represent earth and water, but the red reminds us of the river's force. It's a sacred color."

they weren't. And in low water years, some graves have been exposed, revealing as well the failure of the federal government to live up to many promises made during the taking of tribal land.

The rising water shattered lives, forcing tribal people to adjust to a life up on the prairies, away from the water and shade and comfort of the river bottom. Some of those effects are seen today, in increased rates of alcoholism and unemployment, and cultural struggles that are only now being addressed and fully understood.

"I think many of the problems we have today are because people have lost that connection with the river, with the river wisdom," Lee says. "We have to get back to that. We have to get back to feeling and understanding that power."

Lee promotes that understanding through her writing and teaching, and by introducing her students to the river and its ways. Other more official tribal programs seek a similar return to the river wisdom.

The Cheyenne River Sioux Tribe has begun a native prairie restoration program centered on more than 20,000 acres of rugged river breaks not far from the land Lanniko Lee's family lost to Oahe. The tribe is reintroducing endangered and threatened species, in particular the rare black-footed ferret, and is managing a buffalo herd and wild mustangs as an educational and cultural program aimed in part at connecting young tribal members with their heritage.

It isn't surprising that the project is centered in the Missouri River breaks, a landscape still filled with promise and hope — and for those willing to seek the wisdom of the river, with the power to heal.

"It was a gradual disappearance," Lee says about Lake Oahe rising to swallow her childhood home near the old Cheyenne Agency, located behind her. "It gave us a long time to reflect."

LEFT: An ancient handprint is surrounded by modern graffiti on Medicine Rock, a 40-ton chunk of limestone that originally sat along the Missouri River near the old Cheyenne Agency. Indian legend has it that the numerous hand and footprints embedded in the stone belong to the Great Spirit. Fiercely guarded by local tribes, the rock proved fatal to Captain John Fielner, a topographer and naturalist with General Sully's 1863 expedition. When he attempted to visit it in 1863, Fielner was killed in an ambush. Removed in 1954 prior to the creation of Lake Oahe, Medicine Rock is now located at the Dakota Sunset Museum in Gettysburg.

RIGHT: Michael Claymore releases a tagged black-footed ferret into a prairie dog colony on the Cheyenne River Indian Reservation. Conservation efforts by the tribe here have reintroduced ferrets, bison and wild mustangs to the open prairie.

LEFT: Highway 212 fades into the gently rolling prairie east of Marksville.

RIGHT: The bridge carrying Highway 212 over the Missouri River passes over the former townsite of Forest City, whose foundations and streets now rest beneath the waves of Lake Oahe. In 1890, Forest City entrepreneurs convinced railroad officials to build a spur to the frontier town from nearby Gettysburg, but the endeavor failed after 10 years of inconsistent service.

ABOVE: A reminder of the harsh reality of prairie life sits nestled in the branches of a young tree on the Todd Mortenson ranch near the Cheyenne River.

RIGHT: Branding is a spring ritual in ranch country, uniting neighbors in the spirit of teamwork and camaraderie. Cowboys commence the annual roundup at Todd Mortenson's ranch as the Cheyenne River glistens in the distance. "It's something that I look forward to in the spring," explains Mortenson. "I like to get mine done and then go help everyone else. I don't have to think or plan, I just take orders."

When Roy Houck first heard about a plan to control flooding on the Missouri River and to provide water for irrigation, he knew it involved a dam.

But he had no idea just how much of a dam, or how far the impact of its construction would reach into the central South Dakota terrain, or into his own life and future.

"At first, they were talking about a much smaller dam," Houck remembered back in the late 1980s, a few years before his death. "They weren't talking about anything like what they did."

What they did was monumental. Begun in 1948 and finally finished for official dedication in 1962, Oahe Dam was a masterpiece of engineering and construction that then ranked as the largest rolled-earth dam in the world. Almost 2 miles long and 250 feet tall, it was a packed and sculptured pile of 92 million cubic yards of earth.

When full, Lake Oahe would reach 250 miles to the north, create more than 2,200 miles of shoreline, measure almost 200 feet deep in spots and cover 350,000 surface acres.

That new world of water would nurture remarkable populations of walleyes, northern pike, smallmouth bass and even chinook salmon. Also, the big lake would claim more than 8,000 acres of land that Houck and his family had earned through years of physical sweat and economic endurance.

This is not a unique story in that land was taken, emotions were hot, feelings were hurt and resentment lingered. Houck enlisted the advice and aid of his friend, Sioux Falls lawyer John Murphy, and prepared for battle. But once he realized that the U.S. Army Corps of Engineers could and would take, for what was then deemed a higher public purpose, the rich bottom land and productive pastures in Potter and Walworth Counties, he set about rebuilding his ranch.

In the process, he reshaped his life, and the future of the family ranching operation, in ways he couldn't have imagined before his unpleasant displacement.

With short-term financial help from Murphy and other Sioux Falls investors – and with the eventual financial settlement from the Corps of Engineers – Houck resettled on a 50,000 acre ranch across the Missouri, 30 miles northwest

Buffalo congregate amid endless sky and prairie on the Houck Ranch. The herd, numbering more than 3,000 animals during good years, ranges over 50,000 acres and utilizes about 150 stock dams.

of Pierre. The ranch was in the river breaks, but didn't have the protected bottom lands that were so important to the family's operations west of Gettysburg.

Houck, a former state senator who served two terms as lieutenant governor, tried his well-bred Hereford cattle for a while. But after extensive losses during blizzards, he eventually expanded his experiment with buffalo, which survive winter storms and offer few calving headaches. For a time, Houck's full-time venture distinguished itself as the largest privately owned buffalo herd in the nation, at more than 4,000 head.

The herd gained international attention when Kevin Costner selected the Triple U Ranch as a film location for his blockbuster "Dances With Wolves."

The buffalo herd is smaller now, ranging from 2,500 to 3,000 head. And since Houck's death in 1992, the ranch has been in the strong hands of his daughter, Kaye Ingle – a woman genetically inclined toward wide grasslands and shaggy brown beasts.

People still drive out to the ranch, about 30 miles northwest of Pierre, to see the location of Fort Sedgewick from "Dances With Wolves," and look at the buffalo. Ingle keeps a small herd in a pasture near the driveway to entertain visitors, and she runs a gift shop at the ranch.

Family members have moved the remains of the fort movie set from its original location about four miles from the ranch headquarters to a creek just behind the house.

"At first we gave tours, but we quit that. It got to be too much," Ingle says. "Now they can just walk to the fort, and stop at the gift shop. I don't know why this long after the movie, but people are still interested. They still just kind of show up."

Ingle continues the ranch's innovative economic uses for buffalo, ranging from specialty meat products to trophy buffalo hunts. Hunters come from across the nation and world, and Ingle said German hunters seem particularly interested in the hunts.

The ranch has its own slaughter house, and ships buffalo meat throughout the country. Prices are down, but Ingle hopes new buffalo jerky, buffalo sticks and canned buffalo meat will help stimulate sales.

It isn't an easy living, but it's a good one. Ingle doesn't regret the move forced by the construction of Oahe Dam. And she believes her dad didn't either.

"I think it's been good for us," she said. "I think he'd say it turned out pretty good."

Kaye Ingle pauses at the door of a movie set as Butter heads back to the ranch house. The majority of "Dances with Wolves" was filmed on the expansive Houck Ranch, and these two buildings served as the movie's fictional Fort Sedgewick. "It was really dry," recalls Ingle of the 1989 filming. "They didn't have to do much to make the prairie look brown that summer."

LEFT: Farmer Jeff Weinheimer checks a sunflower field with the help of children Hannah and Ethan west of their Sully County farm. Sunflowers have become a common crop along the Missouri River here, benefiting from irrigation when available.

RIGHT: A flowering prickly pear cactus emerges from parched soil at Fort Sully Game Refuge, nestled in Lake Oahe's "Little Bend." The second Fort Sully functioned near here from 1866 to 1894, serving to protect settlers from Sioux Indians eager to defend their land from encroachment. The original Fort Sully near Pierre operated from 1863 to 1866.

To fly-bitten walleye hunters skimming across Lake Oahe in deep-hulled fishing boats powered by rumbling gas motors, 8 miles per hour is barely idling speed.

But it's absolutely flying to Bob and Sara Hartford. They have a different traveling perspective from the frenetic walleye seekers who scatter across the big lake in search of the latest hot spot.

The Hartfords don't fly — at least not in the literal sense. They sail.

"We're running at about 7 or 8 miles an hour right now, which is pretty good," Bob Hartford says on a sunny July Saturday, sitting comfortably on the contoured teak deck of their 28-foot sailboat, his deeply-tanned hand draped casually across the tiller. "We don't worry about how fast we get someplace. In a sailboat, you're already there."

To sailors like the Hartfords, "there" is a state of mind, of course, an emotional landscape isolated from their jobs in the nearby capital city. But speaking geographically, "there" also is Oahe, an unlikely sea of sailing opportunity surrounded by an ocean of grass.

A hundred years ago, ranchers along the muddy Missouri River would have laughed at the idea of sailing through central South Dakota in anything other than a horse-drawn wagon or a railroad car.

Now, in these parts, that old rascal of a river has been transformed into the widest section of a 350,000-acre lake. And on hot summer days, sails are almost as common as thunderheads on the lower third of Oahe. One of them often belongs to the Hartfords.

"We try to get out on the water three or four times a week during the summer," Sara Hartford says. "Sometimes we go out alone, and sometimes with others. There's a real sailing community around here."

Sailing in central South Dakota hardly competes with that crafty culture on the East and West coasts or even the Great Lakes. And the sailing season here is shortened by prairie winters that can come early and stay late.

But there are sailors up and down the vast reservoir, with a cluster at Spring Creek, a protected harbor on the east shore of Oahe, about 20 miles

Bob and Sara Hartford slice through water near the mouth of Spring Creek in Liberty, *their 28-foot Herreshoff sailboat. Originally commissioned in 1959 for a naval commander in Yokohama, Japan,* Liberty *came back to America in 1960, sailing waters off of Maryland, Virginia, Texas, Florida, the Caribbean and the Bahamas. The all-wood boat was purchased by Bob in 1988.*

north of Pierre. And on this day, the Hartfords leave their rented slip at the Lighthouse Pointe Marina to sail eight or nine miles down the lake, to an exceptionally wide bend in the reservoir called Peoria Flats.

They are showing off both the boat and the lake to a couple of newspaper reporters who are making their maiden sailing voyage on Oahe. It's a silky smooth experience, in a wooden craft built from a design by L. Francis Herreshoff, designer of America's Cup sailboats during the early 1900s.

Double-planked mahogany, teak and sitka spruce, with a 36-foot main mast and 26-foot second, the *Liberty* is a beauty of a boat. Its earthy, natural feel and style seem especially appropriate, seen against the backdrop of blue water and the smoothly undulating river bluffs with their gray faces and brown grass backs.

The boat was just what Bob Hartford wanted to help him adjust to life away from his childhood home in the San Juan Islands, off the coast of Washington state. When he moved to Pierre to work in economic development for the state, and ultimately to become an executive for the South Dakota Music and Vending Association, he fell in love with Oahe right away. It was the closest thing to home the northern plains had to offer.

"I knew I wanted to be on the lake. I knew I wanted a boat, and I knew I wanted a wooden boat. Wood is a lot of work. It requires a lot of care and attention. But wood is so beautiful, it's worth it," Hartford says, handing the tiller over to his wife to stretch his legs, lean back and watch the white sail wrestle with the wind above his head. "On a day like this, in a boat like this, it doesn't matter how fast you're going or where you're headed."

That's because you're already there.

Constant wave action forms narrow channels along the muddy shoreline at Peoria Flats, the widest part of Lake Oahe. The name "Oahe" is taken from a former Indian mission founded here in 1874: "Ti Tanka Ohe," or "the place of the great meeting house."

LEFT: Parched river bottom at Peoria Flats is exposed during the extremely dry summer of 2002.

ABOVE: Low water following a mild winter and increased dam flows during the spring can create ideal growing conditions for weeds such as this young Russian thistle near Peoria Flats.

On the east side of the Oahe Dam powerhouse, an odd-looking gray concrete structure sits, disconnected from the impressive complex of rumbling turbines and functioning towers and electrical webs.

It is a grave marker, of sorts, an engineered relic of a dream that died.

That dream was the Oahe Irrigation Project. And to those who believed fervently in the potential of a massive Missouri River irrigation project, it was a dream to guarantee bumper crops, provide dependable water supplies and revitalize the farms and municipal economies of central South Dakota.

What it brought instead was perhaps the most caustic environmental war in the state's history, a skirmish that left an abandoned pumping station hooked forlornly onto Oahe Dam and a ragged gash that was to be a canal snaking several miles through the grasslands nearby. It also left a lingering wound in the memories and relationships of those who supported the project, and those who opposed it.

Yet, it all seemed to make such simple sense in the beginning. After all, there was the wild Missouri, day after day, rushing through the heart of South Dakota, past parched fields and cracked pastures thirsty for water. On a good year, that river system carried more than 25 million acre feet of water through the state.

For decades, there were those who watched that water flow and saw it as a resource with a higher purpose.

R.B. Hipple was one of those people. He was a man with a wide blue dream, a vision of a landscape transformed by water, by the massive irrigation project he loved and by the belief that man's ingenuity could improve on nature's existing system.

Hipple took that dream to his grave on Thursday, Dec. 21, 2000. At 100 years old, he died a successful and respected newsman and former publisher, a walking history book on South Dakota and its people and places. He was, in fact, a player in history himself, having dined with the great Charles A. Lindbergh when the fabled pilot stopped in Pierre during a 1927 cross-country flight in the *Spirit of St. Louis*.

R.B. helped clear rocks off a grassy landing strip not far from the river where Lindbergh landed. He also noticed that a door handle fell off the plane on landing, and returned it to the pilot.

Years later, as he pushed his ideas to harness and channel Missouri River might, Hipple helped shape

At 99, a year before his death, Bob Hipple had lived a life full of history. He once welcomed Charles Lindbergh and the Spirit of St. Louis *to Pierre, and introduced engineers Lewis Pick and W. Glenn Sloan, who later collaborated to create the 1944 Pick-Sloan Plan, effectively setting in motion the construction of the Missouri River dams.*

history by introducing Lt. Gen. Lewis Pick of the U.S. Army Corps of Engineers in Omaha, Nebraska, to W. Glenn Sloan, an influential engineer with the federal Bureau of Reclamation in Billings, Montana. The connection would lead to the development of federal law and engineering complexities called the Pick-Sloan Plan for water development on the Missouri River system, resulting in five main-stem dams on the Missouri in North Dakota and South Dakota.

And when Oahe Dam itself was dedicated on Aug. 17, 1962 – after almost 14 years of construction – President John F. Kennedy turned out for the celebration. R. B. Hipple, of course, was smack in the middle of it.

He found himself in the middle of the subsequent water war, too, as critics questioned the wisdom of pumping Missouri River water 100 miles east to irrigate up to 750,000 acres in the James River Valley. Suddenly it wasn't a simple question of bringing water to parched land or realizing a dream. It also was about potential damage to the environment, congressional cost-benefit ratios and infringement on the property rights of landowners who would lose their ground to canals and reservoirs.

Affected landowners organized as the United Family Farmers. They were joined by wildlife and environmental interests, and eventually by what became a majority opinion that the Oahe Irrigation Project, estimated in the 1970s to cost $500 million to $1 billion, would do more harm than good.

It made President Jimmy Carter's wasteful-projects list in 1977, a political demotion in its status that eventually led to de-authorization, after $50 million was spent on planning and initial project work.

Now, all that's left is an odd, idle structure, some scratches in the earth and the memory of a grand dream that wasn't meant to be.

A small bay bordering Chantier Creek features calm water within grass-covered breaks — a far cry from the often white-capped, wide stretches of nearby lower Lake Oahe. It was at Chantier Creek that the lumber for Fort Pierre Chouteau was collected in 1822; "chantier" is French for "timber yard."

A Fourth of July thunderstorm rages above the Oahe Dam power plant, providing a stark contrast between natural and manufactured sources of power. Water drained from more than 243,000 square miles – an area almost the size of Texas – passes through Oahe Dam. The dam comprises 2.5 billion cubic feet of earth and 29.7 million cubic feet of concrete and can discharge 436,000 gallons of water per second at its peak. Generating electricity for use in areas of South Dakota, North Dakota, Minnesota, Nebraska, Iowa and Montana, each of Oahe's seven turbines has the capacity to power a city of 100,000 people.

... *Teaching Tolerance* ...

It's still possible to lose yourself in time on LaFramboise Island.

Find a sunny spot of seclusion among the cottonwoods, with the chickadees singing and the cautious footsteps of white-tailed deer crackling somewhere off in the underbrush, and the year could be 1804, or 2004, or anywhere in between.

Most days, regardless of the year, it is a peaceful place, where hikers, bikers, birdwatchers, anglers and bow hunters go to escape the clock.

Yet this place has become a symbol of conflict, of misunderstanding and distrust, and in the minds of some native people, of betrayal. Those feelings took shape in a non-violent protest of occupation on the island that began in March of 1999 and ended more than a year later.

A small and changing gathering of Native Americans from tribes across the United States and Canada gathered on the island, erected a tipi, tents and other shelter, and started a fire that burned, within a reasonable walk from South Dakota's Capitol building, throughout the occupation.

It is a fire that has been burning symbolically on this stretch of the Missouri River for 200 years. In late summer of 1804, the Corps of Discovery, led by Meriwether Lewis and William Clark, entered what is now South Dakota on the extraordinary journey up the Missouri River and on to the West Coast.

During the 54 days it took for the explorers to work their way through the state, they would have their first significant meeting with the tribal people that would become known, in the white world, as the Teton Sioux. This meeting took place at the mouth of the Bad River, which enters the Missouri in the town of Fort Pierre, across the river, west of LaFramboise Island.

And like so much of Indian-white relations to come, this initial meeting was marred by misunderstanding.

With language and cultural barriers to cross, Lewis and Clark's crew stumbled in the complex system of trading and communications that the Sioux, or Lakota, had developed. At one point, guns were drawn, threatening gestures made, cannons trained and arrows notched.

Supporters of the 1999 LaFramboise Island occupation included (from left) Good Nation Woman (Mary Ann McCowan), Grace Brooks, Peggy Sailors and Donna Augustine.

A Lakota chief named Black Buffalo helped bring calm to the meeting. And after a jittery night, the corps returned the next day to feast with Black Buffalo and his people.

"Lewis and Clark stumbled into a terribly complex political and economic situation, one that they were ill-prepared to deal with," says James Ronda, a University of Tulsa professor who has written about the corps' meeting with Indian tribes.

Much the same can be said of white-Indian meetings overall. Misunderstandings frequently led to conflict. And promises made by the federal government were indeed broken. In most meetings between the indigenous tribes and the federal government, the tribes lost.

Those one-sided exchanges went on well into the 1900s, although then they included monetary compensation. When the four Missouri River dams were built in South Dakota from the late 1940s to the early 1960s, more tribal land was lost. The dams of Oahe, Big Bend and Fort Randall flooded 200,000 acres of land belonging to the Crow Creek, Lower Brule, Cheyenne River and Standing Rock tribes. The dams also flooded thousands of acres of non-tribal land.

Congress passed a law in the late 1990s to return some of that land to the tribes, but it also gave some to the state of South Dakota. Tribal leaders at Cheyenne River and Lower Brule supported the gesture, but other tribes did not.

That led to the protest on LaFramboise, an occupation aimed at strengthening tribal sovereignty and respect for treaty rights, and stopping the river-lands transfer. When it didn't stop the return of lands to the state, the occupation withered and was gone.

But the determination of some indigenous people remains. And LaFramboise, that quiet island with a tumultuous past, will always be a symbol of that.

Situated directly between Pierre and Fort Pierre (foreground), LaFramboise Island is connected to Pierre via a narrow causeway. The site where the Bad River enters the Missouri (lower right) made history September 25, 1804, as the place where Lewis and Clark and the Corps of Discovery encountered the Teton Sioux.

LEFT: Sunrise bathes the South Dakota Capitol in golden light, illuminating 92 years of state history. Built in 1910 at a cost of $1 million, "... the building required 18 carloads (railcars) of furniture and 9 carloads of steel fixtures ..." according to a 1910 listing of materials in the Pierre Capital Journal.

RIGHT: Below the Capitol's copper dome, embellished with stained glass windows and painted murals, state lawmakers meet for two months each spring. Here, a group of Sioux Falls businessmen discuss a successful morning meeting with legislators.

A view from the deck of the railroad bridge between Pierre and Fort Pierre shows dozens of fishermen taking advantage of the annual spring walleye spawn. Finished in 1907, the railroad bridge took two years and 200 men to build. The auto bridge spanning the river in the background carries highways 14, 34 and 83 across the Missouri.

The Pierre Governors and their fans participate in a candlelight vigil following their homecoming football game September 14, 2001. The vigil honored victims of the World Trade Center and Pentagon terrorism attacks which had occurred just three days earlier. The Governors lost to the Sioux Falls Lincoln Patriots 14 to 21.

When an injured hawk or eagle or falcon is brought to Dr. Virginia Trexler-Myren's veterinary clinic in Pierre, she immediately goes to work patching a shattered wing or a punctured organ.

She also hopes to repair some misconceptions. Some people hate raptors. Some people hate them enough to kill them. So hawks get shot. Eagles get poisoned. Owls get caught in leg-hold traps.

Many die. Wildlife agents aren't sure how many, because there are so many places in the wild lands of South Dakota for them to fall. Some don't die, however, and are fortunate enough to be found by a wildlife officer or by a hunter or landowner who respects them and the law.

Those survivors will end up in Trexler-Myren's capable hands. And as she works to save the bird, she also hopes to spread the truth about raptors.

"You know, some people have this idea that hawks and eagles are swooping down and picking up lambs and even calves," she says. "That's just so far from reality."

People must remember the actual size of the birds in relation to what they can carry, Trexler-Myren says. Even a large eagle rarely weighs more than 15 or 16 pounds, with a wing span of 8 feet. That's big, but not big enough to tackle most livestock.

"I doubt if that bird could have gotten off the ground with anything more than half a jackrabbit," Trexler-Myren says, gesturing in the direction of a bald eagle placed in her care.

So each day, she fights both the actual injuries of the birds and the lingering misconceptions of what South Dakota Game, Fish and Parks Department Secretary John Cooper calls "the chicken hawk mentality."

Cooper knows about that firsthand. For two decades he was an enforcement agent for the U.S. Fish and Wildlife Service. Although he's a state wildlife administrator now, he never gets far from the field. And he remembers countless examples of the ignorant hatred of raptors.

"To some people, there's no difference between a ferruginous hawk and a red-tailed hawk, or a rough leg or a prairie falcon," Cooper says. "They're all chicken hawks. There's only two kinds of hawks to them: big chicken hawks and little chicken hawks.

Pierre veterinarian Virginia Trexler-Myren checks a golden eagle's healing wing. With an earlier surgery, she repaired the raptor's shattered wing using a steel pin to stabilize the break.

All Creatures
Animal Hospital

A young northern harrier hawk awaits examination at Trexler-Myren's clinic. Only about 12 weeks old, the fledgling still carries a few remains of its youthful down.

They have this image of them swooping down in the farmyard and carting off chickens and livestock and everything else.

"But people have to understand these birds. They're not the devil incarnate. They're part of the ecological system. They have a place, and it's an important one."

The Missouri River has always been a magnet for raptors. That was true before the dams were built, and it still is. When the river ran free, the cottonwood bottomlands and winding river offered prey for all types of raptors.

The dams haven't changed that. And in some cases, they have provided even more food for eagles in particular, because the large open reservoirs and irrigated cornfields nearby attract hundreds of thousands of ducks and geese in the fall.

Those huge concentrations of waterfowl attract falcons and hawks, and clusters of bald eagles. The birds concentrate below dams, roosting in giant cottonwoods. They hunt the big bays of the reservoirs, searching for sick and injured ducks and geese.

In Pierre, Trexler-Myren has a perfect location for her raptor work, in the middle of the state, near heavy raptor concentrations. For her full-time job she runs a small animal clinic. She isn't paid for her raptor rehabilitation work, nor are any of the small group of volunteers, including her husband. But she gets plenty back for her hours spent over the operating table and exercising recovering birds in a 100-foot-by-100-foot covered pen and flyway near Oahe Dam.

Game, Fish and Parks provides the land, water and electricity for the facility. The U.S. Army Corps of Engineers erected the flight pen.

Trexler-Myren provides the dedication and the expertise, as well as the truth about the birds that some people love to hate.

LEFT: A boat takes a slow cruise along the northern shore of Farm Island near Pierre. First documented by Lewis and Clark, the island is across the water from the original site of Fort Sully, built in 1863.

RIGHT: Farm Island is known for the wide variety of recreational opportunities it offers, some of which include boating, water skiing, tubing, fishing, picnicking, sunbathing, and spotting whitetail deer meandering through the cottonwoods.

Horses huddle together to avoid pesky flies in a pasture east of Fort Pierre.

Plumegrass lines a tranquil Missouri River shoreline as dusk settles on the prairie east of Pierre.

Zane Pries can shoot. But then, that comes as no surprise to his grandpa, Roger.

"I'll tell you, it's just amazing. He's a natural," says Pries, a retired Pierre school teacher, basketball coach and former executive director of the South Dakota Wildlife Federation. "If it's in range and he gets a good look at it, it's probably coming down."

Zane is 12 years old as Roger Pries makes that proud evaluation. The two are sharing a patch of soggy roadside real estate a few miles north of Pierre, hunkering down as one flock of Canada geese after another leaves the chow line in a winter wheat field and flies just out of range en route to the next feeding option.

On this day, nothing falls but their expectations. But despite that and the unfriendly weather, the day is hardly a failure. Pries figures any time spent afield with his grandson is good time, regardless of whether shots are fired and goose breasts collected.

"He's my hunting buddy," the elder Pries says.

That means something in the Pries family, where guns and hunting lore have been handed down through generations of South Dakota outdoorsmen. And it means something in river country, where the pursuit of fish and game is a cultural rite of passage, an autumn obsession for thousands and a multi-million-dollar business that, along with sport fishing, drives the economies of towns like Mobridge, Chamberlain and Pierre.

So it has been since the 1950s and 1960s, when the completion of four main stem dams transformed the Missouri into a string of large reservoirs. Besides supporting riverside crop irrigation, the massive lakes act as magnets for thousands of migrating geese coming off the Canadian prairies, heading for steamier southern environs.

Upward of 300,000 Canada may gather on lakes Oahe and Sharpe during November and December. They are attracted by the irrigated cornfields nearby and open expanses of water that often do not freeze until after Christmas, if at all.

And those birds attract thousands of hunters, from across South Dakota and the nation. For a goose hunter interested in lots of birds and high success, it simply doesn't get much better.

That doesn't mean Missouri River goose hunting is without complications. Much of the best private hunting ground near the major concentrations of geese is either leased by individuals or groups, open to the public for a daily fee or locked up by private hunting

Roger Pries shares a laugh with grandson Zane as they sort Canada goose decoys.

clubs. For some hunters, pay-to-shoot operations provide a reliable place to hunt and a reasonably high-quality experience. Likewise, the commercial fees have helped some farmers and ranchers stay on their land.

But the intense level of commercialization also has led to conflicts with hunters who choose not to pay, but instead use public road ditches and section-line right-of-way – legal in South Dakota – to shoot geese as they fly from the Missouri out to feed, or as they move from within large blocks of private ground.

For decades, Roger Pries has fought to defend public access to those right-of-way corridors, just as passionately as some commercial interests have tried to impede it. Guided by Pries, the South Dakota Wildlife Federation was involved in legal action to guarantee the public's access to section-line roads and trails in goose country, an effort that was largely successful.

Pries still has a few spots on private land where he can hunt. But mostly, he hunts the ditches and section-line trails. And in the off season, he still patrols back roads throughout goose country, watching for road blocks or fences across public section lines, or crops planted over the top of them.

Though retired, he can't surrender his investment in public access.

"Really, for the average guy, these section lines, the public right-of-way, they're about all he has left to hunt," Pries says, sharing a sandwich on a section-line trail. "You know, I've watched the commercial thing grow and grow. And I just think when everything else disappears, there still will be right-of-ways, where a guy can take his kids."

Or his grandkids.

A sizeable population of Canada geese winters in the Pierre area each year, taking advantage of open water at Capitol Lake and below Oahe Dam. The migratory destination offers late-season hunting for sportsmen and viewing pleasure for wildlife enthusiasts.

An abandoned one-room schoolhouse is shrouded in early-morning fog along the edge of the Fort Pierre National Grassland. Covering 116,000 acres and managed by the U.S. Forest Service, the public reserve is available for recreation and limited grazing.

Cattails wave along shoreline near the former site of Fort George in eastern Stanley county. The fort, one of the oldest on the upper Missouri River, was built by the Missouri Fur Company in 1819.

LEFT: Male greater prairie chickens participate in their courtship dance, a timeless spring ritual on the Fort Pierre National Grassland. Scurrying stiff-legged in front of the hens, males flare feathers and inflate orange air sacs on their necks, exhaling with a hollow booming sound.

RIGHT: Following a successful spring roundup, hired hands retreat to Jim Schaefer's ranch near Medicine Creek.

LEFT: Paleontology student Rob Meredith carefully brushes layers of mud from a mosasaur fossil near the West Bend Recreation Area. Found in abundance buried in what was once the floor of a massive inland sea covering much of South Dakota, the mosasaur preyed on fish and grew to 40 feet in length. Resembling an alligator with paddles instead of legs, the mosasaur lived between 65 and 90 million years ago. Students from the South Dakota School of Mines and Technology have visited each summer since 1989 to excavate specimens.

RIGHT: A cottonwood trunk rises from the waves in fossil-like fashion after being exposed by low water at the Iron Nation Recreation Area.

With a body that carries the burden of years, injury and illness, Altwin Grassrope slowly picks his way through yucca and prickly pear to sit on a gray boulder above the Missouri.

"Ah, grandfather rock. Let me rest on you for a while," Grassrope says as he settles down on the stone. "You're a good rock."

Good rocks are everywhere on The Narrows, Grassrope's home ground on the Lower Brule Indian Reservation. And good water isn't far away.

To the west 150 yards, the river is wide and blue as it sweeps the shale bluffs below and departs from its southeast journey to run north and northwest, beginning a geographic aberration called the Big Bend.

To the east a mile, as the river returns from its 25-mile digression, the water is a shining ribbon that again heads southeast toward the town of Lower Brule and, a few miles downstream, Big Bend Dam.

In the middle of it all, Grassrope sits on the narrow margin of land that forms the neck of the Big Bend, a dramatic loop in the river's course and a prominent feature in the records of the Lewis and Clark expedition two centuries ago.

The historical significance of the Big Bend – and The Narrows area in particular, where the peninsula is at its skinniest – makes this place especially meaningful in light of the 2004 Lewis and Clark bicentennial.

"That's where Lewis and Clark got off the keelboat and crossed over on foot while the guys doing all the work slogged 25 or 30 miles around the bend," says Cy Maus, an official with the Lower Brule Sioux Tribe. "It's gorgeous up there."

Gorgeous and historic, a combination that attracts visitors from across the nation and world to retrace the trail of Lewis and Clark.

The federal government has estimated that between 2003 and 2007, the Lewis and Clark Trail from St. Louis to the West Coast will attract 25 million visitors. A good share will come to South Dakota's stretch of the Missouri River.

Tribal people here have mixed feelings about that. Some believe it's a chance to further economic development on the reservations. Others fear it's

Altwin Grassrope rests upon "grandfather rock," a boulder in the Narrows that Grassrope's father and grandfather used in spiritual ceremonies. When Lewis and Clark passed this way in 1804, they walked across the Narrows, almost certainly within a few hundred yards of this rock.

just another opportunity for non-Indians to exploit something beautiful and culturally significant.

It's an ongoing dilemma. Tribes need economic development but don't want it at the expense of the environment, their culture or their spirituality.

And the idea of working with any non-Indian form of government is always met with suspicion in Indian country. To some, so is the idea of celebrating the anniversary of Lewis and Clark. It is preposterous to Ambrose McBride, an elder with the Crow Creek Sioux Tribe in Fort Thompson, downstream and across the Missouri from Lower Brule.

"I believe it's not a reason to celebrate," he says. "They kind of spearheaded the invasion of the white race into our country. And look what that did."

Grassrope understands those emotions. Yet he also believes economic development in many forms is crucial to the future of his tribe, and to other tribes along the river.

For that very reason, some tribal members had to make concessions in the development of gaming casinos in Lower Brule and Fort Thompson. Unlike some tribes elsewhere, neither the Lower Brule or Crow Creek tribes are getting rich through non-Indian gamblers. But gaming proceeds help pay for facilities and programs that benefit tribal people.

Both tribes continue to develop farming operations. On the Lower Brule reservation, this includes irrigated fields on the Big Bend itself. The core of the operation is called the Grassrope Unit, in honor of Altwin's family.

Both tribes also work with the state and with area communities off the reservations in an increasingly coordinated effort at tourism promotion.

Grassrope understands those issues, and the inevitable conflicts they will bring. And he believes the tribal values and integrity of the landscape must be preserved, even as some careful forms of development proceed.

Yet he believes there is hope. And in a place like The Narrows visitors and residents alike might come together in a spirit of mutual understanding and peace, he says.

"God knew what he was doing here," Grassrope says. "Someday, we all need to come together. We all need to meet as one."

On a good rock, maybe, and in a good place.

Lake Sharpe wraps around the Narrows in a massive 25-mile bend, creating one of the Missouri's most distinctive natural features. During steamboat days, passengers were allowed to take a mile-long overland shortcut while their vessel made the long journey around the bend, meeting them on the other side.

With the help of great-uncle Cody Russell, Dale La Roche, 3, gets some practice on his pony, Candy, along BIA Highway 10 in Lower Brule. "He just likes to ride, and this is the easiest way to go with him," Russell says.

Lydia Skunk looks for her siblings after 2002 graduation ceremonies at Lower Brule High School. Each of the 19 seniors received star quilts from their families and were honored with eagle feathers and hawk plumes as gifts of accomplishment.

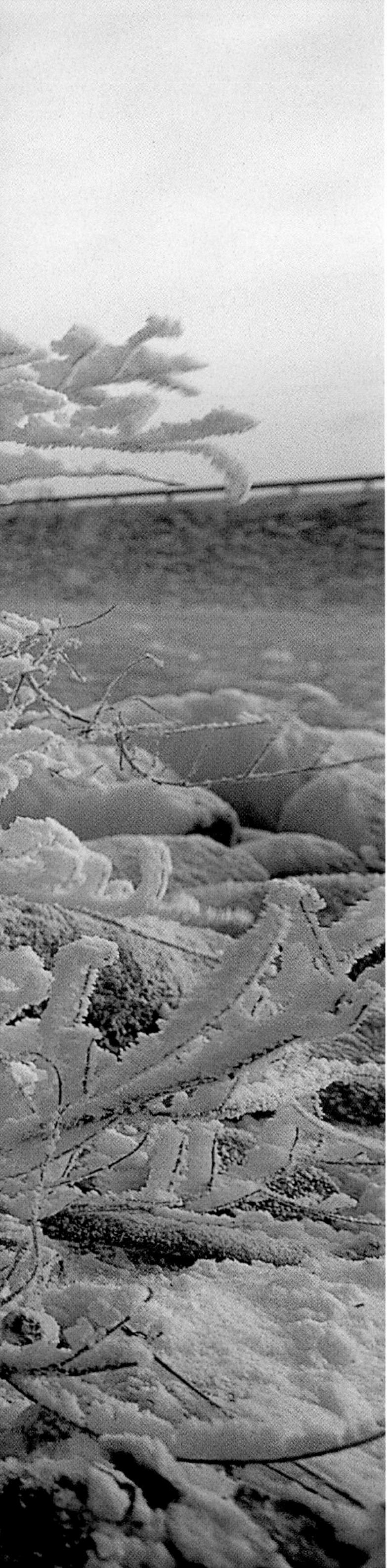

LEFT: The shoreline above Big Bend Dam is laced with ice from fierce sub-zero February winds and open water stimulated by movement around the dam's intakes. The dam is built just south of Fort Thompson, and holds back Lake Sharpe.

ABOVE: Greg Paulson and Jim Baukus take stock of damage from water pressure on one of Big Bend's turbine blades. Each year, water is drained from the concrete caverns behind the dam's floodgates so damage can be assessed and repaired.

LEFT: A common checkered skipper rests atop a gayfeather blossom near Fort Thompson. Its cousin, the Dakota skipper, is a threatened species found in South Dakota.

RIGHT: Ripened wheat awaits harvest as a combine crew makes short work of rolling fields in northeast Lyman County. The ongoing conversion of prairie into farmland during the 20th century has contributed greatly to the siltation of the Missouri River.

LEFT: Crab apples found north of Chamberlain were a summer staple of Indian diet and also enticed Lewis and Clark's crew during their passage through what is now South Dakota.

RIGHT: David Cain, impersonating hunter John Colter, talks with visitors at the mouth of American Creek during a 2001 visit by the Lewis and Clark Discovery Expedition of St. Charles, Missouri. The organization uses a replica 55-foot keelboat to travel the river, stopping to offer tours and educational discussions. "There's nothing better than floating this great river in the same fashion as our forefathers," says Cain. "It's an experience everyone should have."

... *Creating Opportunity* ...

Growing up in Mitchell in the 1950s, Garry Allen never figured he'd end up a Missouri River fishing guide.

Oh, he loved to fish. And he loved to fish the Missouri River. But it wasn't the kind of thing a guy planned on for a profession. Not in central South Dakota, a landscape better known back then for its pheasant hunting, grain farming and cattle production.

"My dad used to take me out to Platte Creek and Pease Creek, to catch crappies. When the reservoir was new, there was great crappie fishing there," says Allen, now a motel owner and fishing guide in Chamberlain. "The walleyes didn't come until later."

But when they came, they came in grand style. As Lake Francis Case, the 107-mile stretch of river backed up by Fort Randall Dam at Pickstown, changed into a reservoir, the fish life changed, too. The paddlefish and pallid sturgeon that depend on moving river and sand bar habitat declined, and the native but scarce walleye exploded.

So did the walleye fishing business. And there was money to be made in walleye fishing, as Allen discovered in 1978.

"I'd moved to Chamberlain so I could fish, and I was managing the motel," Allen says. "One day a couple of guys from Nebraska were staying with us and they couldn't catch any fish. So I took them up to Crow Creek and we caught our limit, 24. Back then it was eight walleyes a day."

When they got back to the motel, the men laid $150 on the table as payment for Allen's guide service. He turned it down.

"I said, 'I'm not going to charge anybody for taking them fishing,'" Allen says. "But $150 was a lot of money back then. And I started thinking about it."

Thinking turned into guiding, and Allen soon ran one of the few walleye guide services operating on the Missouri River in South Dakota. That would change quickly, as the 1980s brought national attention to the emerging walleye fishery on the Missouri River in South Dakota. Good fishermen up and down the river turned to guiding as a full- or part-time job.

And the business communities along the river, especially in towns like Chamberlain, turned more and more to the walleye as a source of revenue. As fishermen came, development followed: more and better boat ramps, new resorts, more guide services, dozens of walleye fishing tournaments offering thousands of dollars in prize money.

Garry Allen trolls for walleye near Chamberlain.

And it wasn't just the walleye. White bass also flourished in the reservoir. And smallmouth bass, one of the sportiest freshwater fish that swims, were stocked – and prospered – throughout the river system.

As surely as it lifted the economy, the sport-fishing surge created conflict and management challenges for the state Game, Fish and Parks Department.

The fishing got so good and the fishing pressure so heavy that over a span of a few years the state lowered the daily walleye limit from eight a day to six and then to four.

In addition, anglers on the river, like those in other state waters, began to face a dizzying assortment of restrictions on which size walleyes could be kept, and which must be returned to the water.

The success of the walleye and the hordes of visiting fishermen led to conflicts between groups representing resident anglers and tourism interests that cater to and attract non-resident fishermen. It's a dispute that continues, as state biologists and wildlife commissioners search for a balance between economic development, recreational opportunity and protection of the river fishery.

It makes Garry Allen's life more complicated, but now he can't imagine doing anything else. Just as his dad, Bruce, inspired Allen to fish, he inspired his own son, Mike. Now Mike and Garry Allen are partners in the motel and guide business.

None of it was planned. But now all of it seems pre-ordained. And Allen expects to spend the rest of his life near the river, and its walleyes.

"You've got great fishing here. It's as good as you can find right here," he says. "I'm here forever."

Greg Scott unhooks a walleye after a successful shoreline cast at the Boyer Game Production Area south of Chamberlain.

ABOVE: A goldenrod spider finds good hunting in a purple coneflower (also known as echinacea) near the White River mouth, southeast of Oacoma. Indians found the root of echinacea to be a helpful numbing substance, using it to soothe pain from toothaches to snakebites.

RIGHT: Sunrise skims parallel hills in the Lindley Game Production Area along the White River mouth.

Ray Baumgart takes a sandwich break while ice fishing offshore from the Buryanek Recreation Area. "There's a dropoff here, and we can catch a lot sometimes," Baumgart explains. "But the sunshine is nice too if the fish aren't biting."

A spring thunderstorm rolls across the countryside west of Academy, blowing dark clouds and tumbleweeds across broken blacktop highway. Quick-moving storms are the bane of boatmen on Lake Francis Case, ruining fishing with choppy waves and lightning.

Otto Qualm gets in position to shoot clay pigeons as father Lee fills the launcher on their Platte farm.

In Lee and Trudy Qualm's little piece of Missouri River paradise, the autumn harvest isn't limited to corn, sorghum and soybeans.

They raise pheasants as well. And those bright, brassy birds of Asian ancestry are as much a cash crop as any grain sucked up in a rumbling combine.

Come mid-October each year, the ringneck harvest begins with shotgun thunder in shelter belts, weed patches and carefully stripped row crops. It is joined by the monetary music of cash registers in pheasant country towns like Mobridge and Pierre, Chamberlain and Platte.

The Qualms grow row crops and small grain on a farm about 12 miles west of Platte, just a couple of miles from the Missouri River. It's a rugged landscape, mixing grassy river breaks and buck brush draws with productive grain fields and undulating cattle pastures. It suits the ring-necked pheasant, a non-native bird brought to South Dakota in the late 1800s.

Within a few years, the newcomer had taken over the the fields and fencerows of central and eastern South Dakota, as well as the hearts of thousands of hunters. From a one-day hunt in Spink County in 1919, the annual pheasant season has evolved into an autumn extravaganza that attracts 80,000 resident hunters a year, along with up to 70,000 shotgunners from other states.

It produces an economic impact of more than $100 million in direct spending, supercharging central South Dakota businesses and communities as they prepare for the economic freeze of winter.

South Dakota has some of the best pheasant hunting on earth. And Missouri River country, particularly the rough mix of grass and grain from Chamberlain to Pickstown, is some of the best of the best.

For decades, however, the economic impact of the autumn hunt missed the farms that produced most of the 5 million pheasants raised in South Dakota during a good year. But by the middle 1980s, farmers, too, were beginning to cash in with pay-to-shoot hunting operations and even hunting lodges.

In some cases, pheasant money literally bought the farm back from the bank after a difficult financial time. And in others, commercial hunting helped struggling farm families survive.

Neither was true of the Qualms when they decided in 1999 to make the thousands of pheasants on their property part of their commercial operation.

"I suppose you could say it was an economic move, but we didn't have to do it," Trudy Qualm says. "My husband just loves hunting. And that was a big part of it."

For Lee Qualm, hunting was a family affair that began with his grandfather, John, during goose and duck hunts on Fort Randall Reservoir when it was the state's top goose water. Pheasants were a natural progression, and as fee hunting became more common, Lee and Trudy talked about taking advantage of the birds on their farm.

"It fits pretty well. I like farming, and I like hunting even better," Lee Qualm says. "We're just getting a piece of the pie."

That kind of development hasn't come without controversy in central South Dakota. Some resident hunters resent the fact that land once open for free hunting now carries a price tag. Some critics of commercial hunting say it ruins the sport and is spoiling a South Dakota tradition.

The Qualms say they're simply making a living doing something they love, and offering a service that people will pay for. If local people are upset, they aren't complaining to the Qualms.

"I think most people want us to succeed. We bring a lot of money into this area," Lee Qualm says.

They run a full-service hunting lodge on their farm, providing meals, hunting dogs, guides and plenty of birds.

"All you have to bring is your clothes and your gun. We take care of everything else," Trudy says.

The lodge building itself is John Qualm's remodeled home. It's called Grandpa's Lodge, and Lee Qualm says that his grandfather will always be part of the operation.

"It probably would have been cheaper for us to tear it down and build something completely new," he says. "But we wanted his home to be part of it. Grandpa had such a love for hunting. He'll always be part of this place."

Especially during the autumn pheasant harvest.

Ringnecks are king in the Platte area, supplementing a sometimes stagnant farm economy. Each fall, out-of-state hunters pump millions of dollars into local businesses and hunting lodges.

LEFT: Fall colors paint the river breaks above Fort Randall Dam.

ABOVE: Sunset highlights ripples on the water at Randall Creek Recreation Area.

LEFT: A bald eagle takes flight from the top of a mighty cottonwood at the Karl Mundt National Wildlife Refuge below Fort Randall Dam. Dozens of bald and golden eagles congregate here each winter to take advantage of open water hunting.

RIGHT: Hard points downstream from the dam prevent heavy releases from eroding one of several mature cottonwood forests along 39 miles of semi-natural river which was designated as the Missouri National Recreational River in 1991. A second, 59-mile designated recreational river runs from below Gavins Point Dam to Ponca, Nebraska.

Most people who study the history of settlement along the Missouri River glean their knowledge from library books or television documentaries.

But for Mike Kirwan, history lives just a mile or two down the road from his Gregory County ranch.

He finds the past in the ruins of a military fort that is slowly returning to the earth in the shadow of Fort Randall Dam. He finds it in a lonesome graveyard on a river-breaks slope nearby and about a mile up the Old Creek Road in the simply sturdy wooden house that has been in his family for seven generations.

"My great-grandfather was a soldier down at the fort, and he got special permission to build this house in 1880. It has to be one of the oldest structures west of the Missouri River in South Dakota," says Kirwan. "It was a really nice house: three bedrooms, a kitchen and living room. And it had a basement."

Clearly Kirwan's great-grandfather was a prosperous man. After fighting in the Civil War and serving on several campaigns against native tribes, Gustav Rieder served in the Black Hills of South Dakota in a fruitless government attempt to keep white miners from entering the area.

He came to Fort Randall after that, in 1874. The fort was then 18 years old, having succeeded Fort Pierre farther up the river as one of the main military enclaves in what had been known as Sioux country.

Fort Randall was, in both symbol and structure, a pronouncement of military control over the northern Great Plains and the beginning of the end for tribal life as native people had known it.

It also was a sign of white expansion and settlement to come, in which Rieder would play a notable role.

"He was a first sergeant at the fort when he took his discharge and got this contract to supply Fort Randall with milk and meat and wood and stuff," Kirwan says. "Because of that, he actually got to build on the military reservation."

Rieder went on to marry Susan Caroll, who had come up the Missouri on a steamboat, along with her mother, to work as a laundress at the fort. They both moved in with Rieder after the marriage, as he built his position in the business community and later became the first mayor of the town of Gregory.

Today he is buried at the cemetery in Gregory, while his wife is buried at the old fort cemetery.

Mike Kirwan holds a snapshot of his great-grandfather and family in front of their 1880 house, which still stands today.

The cemetery is one of the few visible remnants of the fort, the other being the crumbling remains of the chapel. Kirwan often walks the grounds of both, pondering his past and the role his family played in the white settlement of Missouri River country.

"You can still walk through there around the foundations and see where all the buildings were, the officers' quarters and the barracks and things," he says. "It was quite a fort, really.

"And there's still a marker there for my great-grandmother at the fort cemetery."

Kirwan and his wife, Willa Mae, have six children. But none of them is in the farm-ranch operation.

"The farm isn't big enough for anything more than just our family," Kirwan says. "They bought part of dad's land to build the dam. And right next to that old cemetery is part of the old Rieder place."

If the old farm is physically diminished, the memories aren't. And the house stands strong against the elements, even now that it's empty most days.

"My son lived there for several years. And his grandson made seven generations, going back to my great-great-grandmother, who have lived in that house," Kirwan says. "The kids still stay there when they come to visit and it gets crowded. And we had some college kids stay there. The only thing really that has changed is my dad enclosed two open porches. Other than that, it's pretty much the same as it was in 1880."

A piece of history, just a mile down the road.

Sealed with plaster and off-limits to the general public to prevent further deterioration, Fort Randall chapel is the only structure remaining from the 1850s frontier fort. Built in 1875 from highly erodible limestone, the chapel remained mostly intact throughout much of the 20th century. "We used to be able to climb to the upstairs when I was a kid," Kirwan remembers.

In memory of

VIRGINIA JAN

PRATT,

Dau. of

Daniel L. and Gertrude S.

PRATT,

BORN

Dec. 6, 1885.

DIED

Nov. 11, 1887.

LEFT: The gravestone of Virginia Jane Pratt is one of several original stones remaining in the Fort Randall cemetery. A common cause of death was illness or injury, but in the early days of the fort soldiers also fell victim to enterprising Indian war parties. In a letter dated June 13, 1875, Fort Randall soldier H. B. Smith wrote to his cousin Fred in Oxford, New York: "I know it is dangerous to go out side of the camp half a mile alone but I do not go that far ... I was out the other day and had two bullets whiz pretty close. my ears dident like it much but one thing I always did say and will stick to it that is I wont die before my tiem comes no matter what kind of row I get into, I will tell you Fred if you could be in some of the places I have been out here and look at a camp of Indians having a war dance with white People feet and hands cut off and stuck up on poles and the whooping going on it would make you feel a little so so you know what I mean."

RIGHT: The intersection of Lewis Avenue and Clark Drive in Pickstown boasts a grassy lane and a terminated sidewalk. Though Pickstown was created to house Fort Randall Dam construction workers, many of the town's occupants left after the work was completed in 1956. It wasn't until the 1990s that the town's population began to rise again, thanks to a vibrant hunting and fishing industry.

Ice shards collect along the Missouri River shore west of Marty during the spring ice breakup. Prior to the creation of the dams, ice floes wreaked havoc with river communities and sometimes destroyed steamboats when their captains were caught unaware.

Colorful chalkstone bluffs tower over stands of sumac near Greenwood. The rock is common along the Missouri River banks from Chamberlain to Yankton.

Soybeans get a reprieve from hot and dry conditions through the aid of an irrigation pivot near the mouth of Choteau Creek. Though most crops on the Missouri bottom thrive because of irrigation, murky runoff returns to the river with tons of silt.

From the backyard of his home in Springfield, Norm Schelske can watch the Missouri River return to its old, cantankerous ways.

It is clogging the upper end of Lewis and Clark Lake with tons of silt, shaping chutes and islands and shallow backwaters with haphazard ferocity. Now willows grow where water skiers once sliced across blue waters, and white-tailed deer strut and stamp where catfish and sauger once swam.

It's good for ducks and other wildlife, but not so good for a community that thought the construction of the Missouri River dams would turn it into a boating and recreational destination. That happened, but only for a few years.

"I remember when this was a lake. Now it's a marsh," says Schelske, looking down over a patchwork of water, sandbar, cattails and willows. "And there's nothing we can do to stop it."

The force is relentless. The Niobrara River pours into the tail end of Lewis and Clark a few miles upstream from Springfield, bringing with it 5 million tons of silt a year. The Missouri, like all rivers, is an earth-mover by nature. It uses that fine-grained soil carried by the Niobrara as it always has, to clog and build, shape and renew banks and bars and islands, a process that is causing problems throughout the system of Missouri River reservoirs and in the flowing stretches between dams.

Most major tributary streams for the Missouri in South Dakota have formed deltas of sediment where they enter the river and its reservoirs. That's true near the mouth of the White River, the Bad River, the Cheyenne and others.

In some instances, that clogging causes water to back up on private land, flooding farm fields and killing cottonwood trees crucial to bald eagles and other wildlife. In Pierre and Fort Pierre, the U.S. Army Corps of Engineers has had to purchase some homes because of flooding related to silt build-up.

In other areas, the agency bought flowage easements from landowners to help compensate for damage and lost land productivity.

The solution is complicated. Delta formation is a fact of life in dam construction. Before the dams were built, the Missouri River carried a silt load of 175 million tons a year at Omaha, Nebraska. Because of the settling effect in the reservoirs, that load is now 25 million tons.

That means the water rushing from the dams these days is clear and even hungrier than before, lifting tons of sandbars and tearing and pulling at river banks. Some riverside farmers in the Vermillion and Yankton areas have lost acres of corn and soybean fields to the river.

Most try to fight it with makeshift rip-rapping operations that are expensive, aesthetically questionable and marginally effective.

The lost sediment dumped in the reservoirs is ruining some spawning areas for game fish and degrading popular walleye fishing spots. But it has benefits, too. The sediment build-up near Springfield has created a semblance of the old Missouri, with its changing channels and bars and shallow backwaters. That has been good for nesting piping plovers and least terns, as well as for native river fish including the paddlefish and pallid sturgeon.

It also has provided marvelous duck hunting opportunities and productive, if challenging, fishing spots for a variety of species, including but not just limited to the popular walleye.

"You have an area down there that is actually acting like the old Missouri River," says Corps of Engineers biologist Casey Kruse. "It's a fantastic ecosystem."

It just isn't what most people in Springfield had in mind 40 or 50 years ago.

After Gavins Point Dam was constructed about 25 miles downstream in 1955, the river just west of Springfield was the recreational mecca promised by federal officials years earlier. Cliff Stone, now a reservoir biologist with the state Game, Fish and Parks Department in Chamberlain, was a high school student in Springfield back then. He remembers water skiing from the east bank of the reservoir to the west.

Now you'd need an amphibious vehicle and plenty of determination to make that trek. The river is taking back some of what it lost to the dams, and in the process finding much of its ancient self.

In spite of the dams and in some cases because of them, it's doing what rivers do, and what they always have done.

A great blue heron glides over a sea of plumegrass that has grown on solid sediment near Running Water. Between the town of Springfield and the Niobrara River mouth, the Missouri River has silted itself nearly shut, forming several shallow, winding channels reminiscent of the pre-dam Missouri.

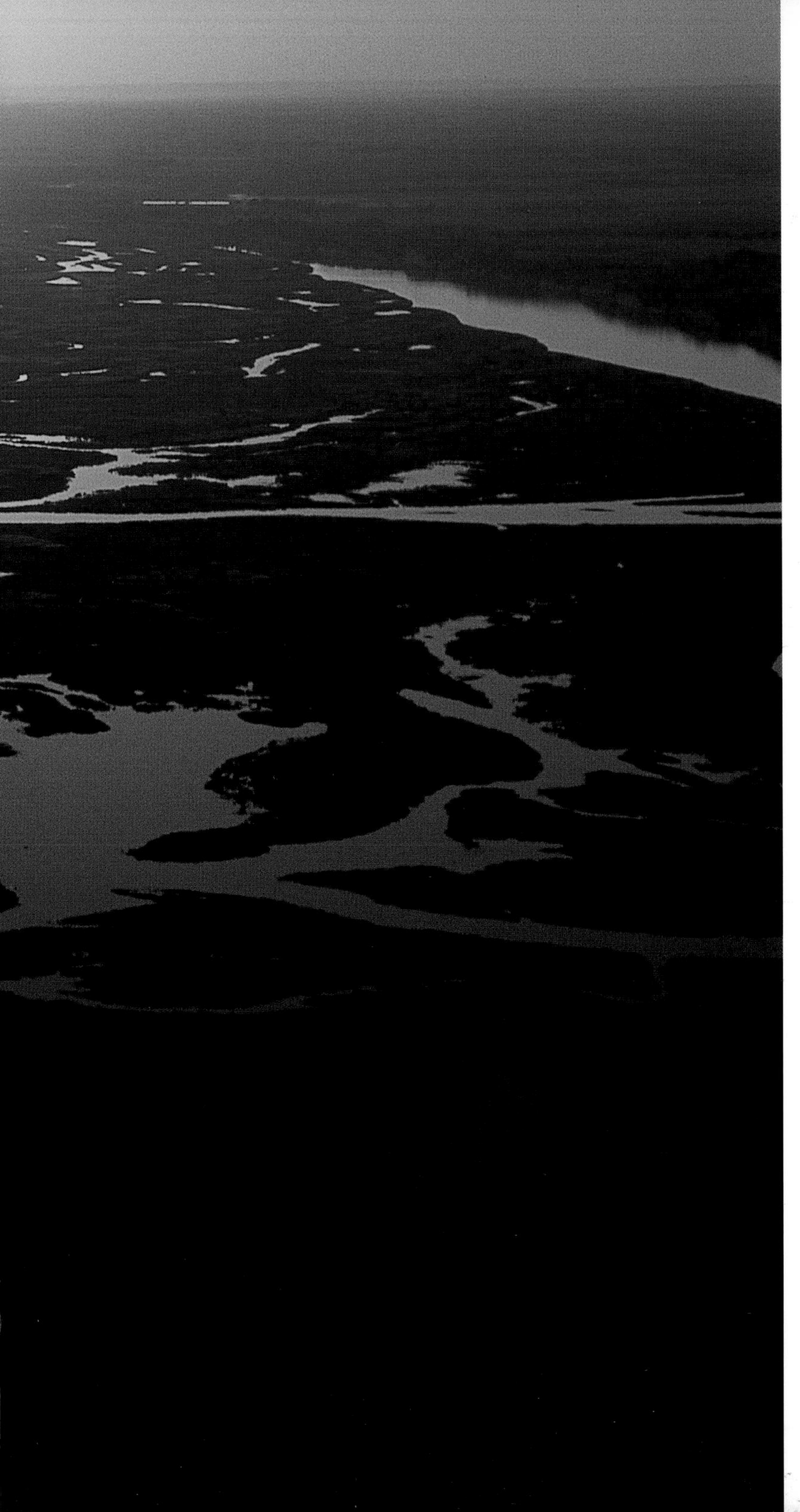

The Missouri River is transformed into dozens of winding channels and shallow backwaters between Springfield and Running Water. The vast network of marsh, sandbars and sediment is a result of silt deposited by the Niobrara River, which empties into the Missouri upstream.

... *Inspiring Survival*

Lewis and Clark Lake is famous for its visitors. The most obvious of them came to this stretch of forested river bluffs in what is now extreme southeast South Dakota two centuries ago, before Gavins Point Dam or the 25,000-acre lake it created.

Capts. Meriwether Lewis and William Clark brought three dozen men and one dog up the Missouri River during their historic mission in 1804.

They met with Yankton Sioux leaders on what is now known as Calumet Bluff. And they began a tradition of exploration that continues today, in ways much less rigorous but nonetheless vital to this region and its people.

Calumet Bluff continues to be a meeting place. Now it supports the Lewis and Clark Visitors Center, a U.S. Army Corps of Engineers facility located on the bluff above the river and immediately downstream from Gavins Point Dam.

Gavins Point is the last of six massive hydroelectric dams on the Missouri River in the Dakotas and Montana. It is also the focal point for a recreational destination that is unequaled in South Dakota east of the Black Hills.

Each year, close to 2 million visitors come to Lewis and Clark Lake, the downstream area of Gavins Point Dam and the collection of campgrounds, hiking trails, boat ramps and related recreational spots.

The long reach of Lewis and Clark is clear. The state's main recreation area just above the dam attracts more than 1 million visitors a year on its own. Throw in other state and federal recreational areas, as well as those operated by the state of Nebraska on the opposite shore, and the total nears 2 million.

By comparison, the record annual visitation at the Mount Rushmore National Memorial, South Dakota's most prominent tourist attraction, is 2.7 million.

On a typical summer day, you'll find anglers, hikers, boaters, swimmers, archers, bikers, sailors, birdwatchers and divers within a few miles of Gavins Point. State and federal parks officials expect the lake above and river below the dam to attract record numbers of visitors during the bicentennial celebration of the Lewis and Clark expedition.

With good reason, says Doug Hofer, parks and recreation director for the South Dakota Game,

A group of teens from Columbus, Nebraska, roasts marshmallows over a fire pit in the Lewis and Clark Recreation Area campground.

Fish and Parks Department in Pierre.

"This is not only South Dakota's most popular recreation area, it is one of the premiere recreation areas in the entire Midwest region," Hofer says.

At the center of the action is the Lewis and Clark Marina, located on the South Dakota shore just above Gavins Point Dam. Its 386 individual slips are home to everything from relatively modest fishing boats to 46-foot sailboats.

Lewis and Clark is the state's busiest sailing water. About 40 percent of the boats operating out of the marina are sail-driven. About a third are owned by Yankton area residents, but one in four owners lives in Omaha, Nebraska, along with considerable numbers from Sioux Falls and Sioux City.

Anglers come to the lake, too, for its walleye and sauger, catfish and bass. And just below Gavins Point Dam, the state allows a limited snagging season on paddlefish, an ancient river species that, like the endangered pallid sturgeon, suffered dramatic population losses after the dams and the changes they brought to the Missouri.

As those and some other native species declined, walleyes and other popular sport fish exploded in the new lake environment. Fishing, sailing and skiing now anchor the recreational world at Lewis and Clark. And Hofer says modern-day explorers will discover a river landscape that isn't as wild as 200 years ago but that might, in many ways, be just as inspirational.

"As people follow the Lewis and Clark Trail to celebrate that journey, they will find experiences similar to what Lewis and Clark and their men experienced," Hofer says. "They can camp and fish and boat and swim and observe nature. In addition, they can explore new possibilities, like bicycling, horseback riding and rollerblading.

"These new explorers can't experience the same world that Lewis and Clark knew. But they can feel the same sense of freedom and adventure."

Visitors here always have.

Visitors flock to one of several beaches bordering Lewis and Clark Recreation Area on a sunny Saturday afternoon. In the distance, boats and personal watercraft dance on the waves outside the Lewis and Clark Marina.

Standing between tanks at the Gavins Point National Fish Hatchery, Herb Bollig holds a living piece of the prehistoric past and symbol of a hopeful future.

The 9-inch long, shark-like fish with the armored shell writhes in slow motion as Bollig gently slips it back in the water, where it merges into a dark gray cloud of fins and motion.

"You can tell by looking at it that it's a river fish. And it's a very primitive fish, sort of a living dinosaur," says Bollig, hatchery manager for the U.S. Fish and Wildlife Service facility along the Missouri River near Yankton. "It did quite well in the old Missouri. But it just had trouble adapting when all the changes came to the river."

Those changes included a series of six main-stem dams, four of which were built in South Dakota. It also included the transformation, and many would say degradation, of the winding, unpredictable river into a channelized shipping channel from the Elk Point area all the way down to the Mississippi River at St. Louis, Missouri.

These drastic alterations brought much good to river country, including flood control, beneficial water supplies, hydroelectric power, irrigation and an explosion in the walleye and other sport fish that help power the economy in central South Dakota.

But they literally strangled the life cycle for many native wildlife species, the pallid sturgeon in particular.

For eons, pallids prospered in the ever-changing river channels of the Missouri, adapting perfectly to the silt-laden water that sliced through sand flats and wound around gravel bars. Its reproductive cycle fit with the chilly floods of spring that faded to the sluggish warm flows of summer.

But less than 50 years after dam building began on the Missouri, the pallid sturgeon was placed on the federal endangered species list. Now it's Bollig's job, and the work of other fisheries experts in state and federal wildlife agencies, first to make sure it avoids extinction and second, to develop a viable population of pallids in stretches of the Missouri where it has been all but lost.

Toward these goals, fisheries teams netted a few surviving adult pallids in areas of the Missouri and its tributaries. These fish were used for egg collection and artificial propagation programs that began producing baby sturgeon for restocking into the river.

Pallid sturgeon are nursed into adolescence at Gavins Point Fish Hatchery. The prehistoric fish are an endangered species, a result of changes in their Missouri River habitat since the installation of the dams.

Fisheries biologist Craig Bockholt checks a beaker of bass fry netted from one of 36 hatchery ponds. Each season, biologists here grow bass, walleye, pike, perch, trout and up to 11 other species to be stocked into South Dakota's lakes, rivers and streams.

"When we started, we didn't even know if we would find any sturgeon to work with. And even then, we had so much to learn," Bollig says.

But they learned. And Gavins Point became one of the nation's centers for pallid sturgeon revival. It works with federal and state hatcheries and fisheries teams in other Missouri River states, providing young pallids for stocking and brood fish for future production.

It's one example in a network of programs up and down the Missouri to help rare wildlife species that were hurt by the system of dams. The prehistoric paddlefish, a lumbering river fish with a pronounced spatula-shaped snout, was kept off the endangered species list at least in part by programs to spawn and restock baby paddlers.

Two shorebirds weren't quite so lucky. The interior least tern winters along the Gulf of Mexico and on Caribbean islands, and the piping plover spends the cold months primarily along the Gulf Coast.

But both return to South Dakota and to the Missouri River system in the spring, searching for nesting sites on open sand and gravel bars that were so common in the old Missouri River.

Many of those areas have been swallowed by dams and diminished by the artificial flows required to maintain a shipping corridor downstream.

The key to survival for terns and plovers is water flow and sand bars. "The Missouri River has been operated in a way that was out of sync with the life cycles of these birds," says Casey Kruse, part of a Corps of Engineers recovery team for terns and plovers that also includes biologist Greg Pavelka.

Kruse and Pavelka and the work they do are signs of change in river management. And wildlife experts and river advocates hope the changes will continue toward water control policies that are more beneficial to rare wildlife species.

In a biological opinion issued in 1999, the Fish and Wildlife Service said that such changes are crucial to the survival of the terns and plovers, and the pallid sturgeon.

Now the fish, and the birds, and the people who love them, are waiting to see if human river managers will finally unleash at least enough of the old river spirit to make that happen.

LEFT: Growing paddlefish is a delicate process. Each spring, eggs are extracted from female paddlefish captured in Lake Francis Case. Kept in beakers with continuous water movement and consistent temperatures, the eggs hatch and the paddlefish fry begin a diet of zooplankton. While many eggs and fry are transported to other hatchery and research facilities, 25,000 fish are kept for release back into Lake Francis Case after reaching a viable size.

RIGHT: Mark Doty (left, with pole) gets help hauling a 58-pound paddler from the Gavins Point Dam tailrace, where anglers gather each fall to snag the fish during a special season.

LEFT: A piping plover fledgling sprints across a Missouri River backwater, while nearby an interior least tern nest, RIGHT, lies camouflaged on a sandbar east of Yankton. Every spring, U. S. Army Corps of Engineers biologists monitor plovers and terns on dozens of sandbars, counting nests and successful hatches. If water levels are low during the initial nesting period, then dams are often ordered to limit water releases throughout the birds' gestation to protect fragile nests close to the water's edge. The federal government lists plovers as a threatened species and terns as endangered.

LEFT: The Yankton Daily Press & Dakotan *is the state's oldest continuous newspaper. First published in 1861 as* The Weekly Dakotian, *it coincided with the inception of Dakota Territory and actively reported events of the 1862 Santee Sioux Uprising.*

RIGHT: Yanktonians celebrate Riverboat Days with a parade. Started in 1984, the event commemorates Yankton's rich riverboat history, which dates to the early 1820s when steamboats first traveled upstream to the frontier outpost.

EY'S
BAR
MEREDITH'S
JEWELRY
MARLOW & J

Migrating snow geese soar above a submerged sandbar near Goat Island west of Vermillion. Each spring, more than 3 million snow geese following the Central Flyway from the Gulf Coast to Canada visit the Missouri River in South Dakota.

To Jim Heisinger, the Missouri River has been a creature of split personalities.

The river he knew while growing up in Jefferson City, Missouri, was an angry being that ran deep and dark and fast between confining levees built and maintained by the U.S. Army Corps of Engineers.

It was not a friendly place, nor one to offer inspiration or solace.

"It was really a dangerous river where I grew up," says Heisinger, a retired biology professor, department head and associate dean at the University of South Dakota in Vermillion.

"It was not really a river where you'd go to fish or to canoe. I went to smaller rivers and streams for that."

All of that would change when Heisinger was a young man looking for a place to teach biology. He found it in Vermillion with USD.

And he found what he considers to be the real Missouri River.

"When I came here and first saw the Missouri here, it was such a different river than the one I'd known," Heisinger said. "It was just beautiful. I thought, 'This is an outdoor jewel.'"

It's a flawed jewel, of course, with river banks littered here and there with irregular riprap and private homes that range from classy to tacky. That's true even in a 59-mile stretch of river from Gavins Point Dam downstream to Ponca, a part of the Missouri National Recreational River. Aesthetic degradation is especially poignant there.

But there also are wonderful stretches of semi-wild water, meandering between cottonwood forests and winding around islands and bars in ways similar to what Lewis and Clark knew 200 years ago.

It's those river gems which have helped hold Heisinger in Vermillion over the years, and still draw him to the water regularly.

In 1976, he moved north of town, to a country home on a ridge above the Vermillion River. The small tributary of the Missouri has helped strengthen Heisinger's connection to the bigger water just a few miles downstream.

"A really good day for me is to put my kayak in the Vermillion River, float down to the Missouri and then float on down to Ponca State Park," Heisinger says. "I don't go beyond Ponca much, because then you get into that channelized portion of the river."

Heisinger saw enough of that river as a kid. It is uninspiring water, and he wants something else for his

Jim Heisinger stops his kayak along a scenic stretch of national recreational river west of Vermillion.

Cottonwood groves tower high above the sandy shoreline south of Vermillion. The cottonwood has a firm place in Missouri River history, having provided such necessities as shelter for frontier settlers and fuel for the 19th century steamboat industry, along with fulfilling a multitude of uses for Indian tribes.

kayak trips. He wants the shallow backwaters and mysterious chutes, the shifting sandbars and willow woods, the cottonwood forests that support a world of wildlife and native plants. He likes the swirling, changing currents and the mysterious creatures they hide.

And his low-riding kayak gets him close to the wildlife in and along the river without disrupting it.

"I remember once I ran over a beaver in the kayak. I was going through a backwater and I felt something as I slid over the top of it," Heisinger says. "I said, 'What the heck was that?' and looked back, and there was the beaver, looking at me like 'what the heck was that?'"

The design of the kayak makes him feel connected to the river, a part of it all as no other water craft can, Heisinger says.

"You're so low down, right in the water, and it's easy to almost imagine yourself as part of the water," he says. "I get into that sensation that I'm really some sort of water beast myself."

He's a mild-mannered water beast, a slender, willowy man with a gentle disposition that hardens on the subject of protecting the river.

Three years after his retirement, Heisinger is more active politically than at any time in his career. He is a leader with the Living Rivers Group of the Sierra Club, which works to protect the remaining native stretches of the river.

"I guess I decided to get more involved in those issues," Heisinger says. "I'd kind of been on the sidelines, I guess."

Which is no place for a river beast to be.

ABOVE: Smooth sumac bursts with vibrant color across the lower Missouri River valley each autumn, creating a rich red contrast with other deciduous foliage.

RIGHT: The gradual peak of Spirit Mound, one of the few identifiable South Dakota landmarks noted by Lewis and Clark during their journey, breaks the monotony of flat prairie north of Vermillion. After climbing to the summit on August 24, 1804, amid warnings from local Indians that the location was inhabited by 18-inch devils, Lewis and Clark were treated to an extraordinary view. Clark later wrote, "... from the top of this Mound we beheld a most butifull landscape; Numerous herds of buffalow were Seen feeding in various directions ..."

The late Ole Olsen's powder horn and rifle were treasured tools of his re-enactment role depicting Pierre Dorion, a trapper and interpreter hired by Lewis and Clark during their Missouri River expedition. For many years prior to his death in 2000, Olsen was instrumental in organizing the annual Lewis and Clark Heritage Days in Elk Point.

Ben Gries and Melissa Mau keep warm under a blanket during a late afternoon track meet in Elk Point. The track is just a stone's throw from Heritage Park, a Lewis and Clark campsite believed to be the location of the first election to take place west of the Mississippi on August 22, 1804. The election resulted in Patrick Gass succeeding the deceased Sergeant Charles Floyd.

From the shoreline at Nebraska's Ponca State Park, with a rolling backdrop of oak and basswood and linden and cedar, Paul Hedren faces the Missouri River with a sense of joy and sadness.

It is here that the 59-mile stretch of the Missouri National Recreational River ends and the navigational canal that will run for 750 miles to the Mississippi begins.

It is here that the semi-wild Missouri gets squeezed from a self-determined being, with backwaters and sandbars and snags and eddies, into a creature of commerce and convenience.

It is here that the last vestige of the old Missouri ends.

"It's pretty stark, pretty dramatic," says Hedren, superintendent of the recreational river for the National Park Service in O'Neill, Nebraska.

"You look to the left and see this wild, snaggy, dynamic river. Look right and you see the canal. You rejoice this way and cry that way."

Not everyone cries, of course. Some see the value in a predictable Missouri, corralled by earthen dams and dikes and rip-rapped shoreline, dredged to provide a reliable canal for barges and their cargo moving from Sioux City, Iowa, to St. Louis, Missouri.

Riverside farmers have prospered by this predictability. Main Streets that once flooded in the spring are now generally safe. Municipal water supplies are secure, power plants cooled and maintained, irrigation systems flush.

But the Missouri River, in every meaningful sense, is gone. It runs dark and cool and fast and mostly sterile from here to the Mississippi.

The comparison here – the wild old river independence on the left, the deflated acquiescence on the right – is as telling as any contrast along the 2,341-mile river journey from Three Forks, Montana to St. Louis.

Just a few miles downstream, the river will end its 497-mile affair with South Dakota's landscape, wildlife and people. It will collect the sluggish brown Big Sioux River below a crumbling bluff just north of Sioux City.

Between those dissimilar streams, South Dakota ends in a prominent point of land connected to one of the wealthiest counties in the nation.

Southern Union County is an aberration thanks to

Resource Manager Wayne Werkmeister, left, and Recreational River Superintendent Paul Hedren tour the river near Ponca State Park.

Frost glistens on a spiderweb spun in the thick underbrush across from Ponca State Park. The second Missouri National Recreational River designation ends its 59-mile stretch near here. A little farther downstream, the river becomes completely channelized all the way to St. Louis.

the prosperity brought by Dakota Dunes, a cluster of corporate headquarters, a professional-tour golf course and luxury homes that grew out of fertile river-bottom soil and South Dakota's low corporate tax burden.

It is an exceptionally opulent landscape by South Dakota's humble, agrarian standards. It is also a floodplain that, before the Missouri River dams and dikes and canals, couldn't have survived.

It's ironic that just a few miles upstream the Missouri makes its last statement of independence before falling into a brown role of subservience. It is a vital statement that Hedren and others with a love for the old river ways are committed to preserving.

The 59 miles of semi-natural river from Gavins Point Dam to Ponca, along with a similar 39-mile run below Fort Randall Dam upstream, are as valuable as any gem, as much in need of preservation as any shorebird or fish or soaring raptor.

"There's much to love about both of those stretches," Hedren says. "This lower stretch is a bit more developed, and it doesn't spread out as much as the upper stretch. But it, too, is breathtaking.

"You can still come around a bend and be in the middle of two miles of river that seem hardly touched by man at all."

Hedren and his staff are increasingly involved in protecting those qualities. For years a recreational river in name only, the two designated stretches are finally being recognized as the national treasures they are.

The National Park Service is adding staff, erecting interpretive stations, deploying rangers and enforcing laws and regulations designed to protect the integrity of the river.

It has taken decades to reach this point. And it's still a bit-by-bit process. But it's as certain as the perpetual force of the river itself.

"Our goal is pretty simple," Hedren says. "Let's let the river be the river."

Now and forever.

LEFT: A stand of plains coreopsis graces renovated prairie at the Adams Homestead and Nature Preserve west of Sioux City. The preserve, donated from the original 1872 homestead of Stephen Adams, attracts visitors to its serene trails and native plant species, and is "a place for inner renewal," say granddaughters Mary and Maud Adams.

RIGHT: Flower girl Haylee Twillman, 4, catches a cool breeze before heading back into the Dakota Dunes clubhouse for the reception celebrating her aunt Mindy Musselman's wedding to Chris Miller. Behind her, the Missouri River and the 18th green of Dakota Dunes Golf Course soak up the evening sun.

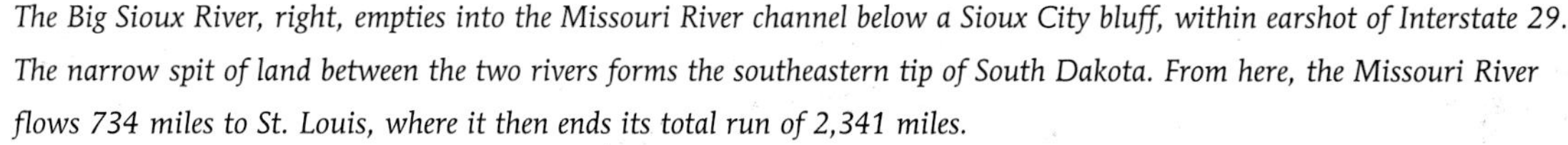

The Big Sioux River, right, empties into the Missouri River channel below a Sioux City bluff, within earshot of Interstate 29. The narrow spit of land between the two rivers forms the southeastern tip of South Dakota. From here, the Missouri River flows 734 miles to St. Louis, where it then ends its total run of 2,341 miles.

Acknowledgements

As always, there are many people to thank during the course of producing a book. South Dakotans are known for their helpfulness and hospitality, and the experience we had making *The Missouri* proved that point very well.

We would like to thank Bernie Hunhoff for writing a wonderful, heartfelt foreword. Bernie is a wealth of knowledge, and I found more than one idea for this book hidden in back issues of *South Dakota Magazine*. Yanktonians should be very proud to call this native son their own.

Our spouses, Jodi and Mary, deserve kudos. It's one thing to be married to people like us, but quite another to tolerate the lengths we go to in order to document South Dakota, our favorite subject. Your ongoing support is invaluable.

Thanks to all the people pictured and mentioned in *The Missouri*. Your willingness to share your stories with the rest of us brings better understanding to an often misunderstood river.

Many people – photo subjects, story sources and river officials – are to be thanked: Garry Allen; Assumption of the Blessed Virgin Mary Church at Kenel; Gordon & Marilyn Atkinson; Donna Augustine; Jim Baukus; Ray Baumgart; Sylvan Beautiful Bald Eagle; Rev. Steve Biegler; Brian Blair & campers; Craig Bockholt; Herb Bollig; Steve Borah; Grace Brooks; David Cain; Capital City Air Carriers of Pierre; Cheyenne River Sioux Tribe; Michael Claymore; John Cooper; Crow Creek Sioux Tribe; Mark Doty; Falcon Aviation of Yankton; Fort Pierre National Grasslands officials; Ajay Fox; Bobbi Lynn Gaukel; Altwin Grassrope; Ben Gries; Charlie Hamer; Dave Hansen; Harold's Photo Centers of Sioux Falls; Bob & Sara Hartford; Mary Alice Haug; Paul Hedren; Jim Heisinger; Bob Hipple; Doug Hofer; Paul Horsted; Roy Houck; Kaye Ingle; Gordon Iseminger; Liz James; James Johnson; Bob Karolevitz; Michael Kirwan; Casey Kruse; Dale La Roche; Gary Larson; Gene & Carol Latza; Lanniko Lee; Lower Brule High School Senior Class; Lower Brule Sioux Tribe; Gary Marrone; James Martin; Melissa Mau; Cy Maus; Ambrose McBride; Mary Ann McCowan; Rob Meredith; Jerry Miller; Mindy & Chris Miller; Todd Mortenson & gang; Alison Nelson; Joe Night; Monsignor William O'Connell; Oahe Vet Hospital of Mobridge; Dave Ode; Dianne & Doug Olander; Ole Olsen; Herald Park; Greg Paulson; Greg Pavelka; Pierre Governors Football Team; Virginia Jane Pratt; Roger & Zane Pries; Tom Pringle; Lee, Trudy & Otto Qualm; James Ronda; Cody Russell; Elaine St. John; Peggy Sailors; Jim Schaefer; Ron Schauer; Norm Schelske; Jim, Priscilla, Russ & Vickie Schott; Harold Schuler; Greg Scott; Jack Shillingstad; Virginia Driving Hawk Sneve; South Dakota Department of Tourism; South Dakota Department of Game, Fish & Parks officials; Ken Stach; Standing Rock Sioux Tribe; Cliff Stone; Bobbi Three Legs; Kolt Tiger; Virginia Trexler-Myren & Tessa Myren; Haylee Twillman; U.S. Corps of Engineers officials; U.S. Fish & Wildlife officials; Jeff, Tomi, Ethan, Hannah & Avery Weinheimer; Wayne Werkmeister; Charlie Whitney; Phyllis Wise; George Wolf; Terry Woster; and Yankton Sioux Tribe.

And for those we have inadvertently forgotten to mention, please accept our apologies ... you know who you are!

Production Notes

The idea behind this book is to show people that there are interesting things to see within the gaps left by most Lewis and Clark books that follow the Missouri River through South Dakota. Although it isn't specifically about Lewis and Clark, *The Missouri* does illustrate the route they traveled through our state and puts a modern spin on the people and places now found in their wake. There are just too many interesting stories to tell between the "important" locations and events described in their journals: Patrick Gass' election, the hike to Spirit Mound, meeting the Yanktons, arguing with the Teton Sioux and experiencing Arikara hospitality. So, instead of making a photography book about the Missouri River's past, it seemed more fitting to illustrate the great things found here today.

Kevin was the only person we ever considered asking to write this book. His knowledge of the river and its people is unmatched, and it was a great pleasure to work together again after my five-year absence from the *Argus Leader*. I first approached him about the project in 1998, and he was eager to help from the beginning. We pored over a handful of formats and outlines over the next couple of years, and finally agreed that Jodi's idea to use several short profiles of specific people and issues was the best answer. Kevin and I combined our lists of ideas and narrowed the subjects into the final selection. After two years of gathering content, the photographs and stories were brought together in mid-2002 and arranged as you see them here. I researched and wrote the cutlines while Jodi designed and edited layouts. After the three of us conferred over the final product, it was sent to press in August.

This book isn't meant to be the most comprehensive collection of Missouri River stories and facts available. It is simply a collection of photographs and details we hope will make the river more interesting to South Dakotans and those who visit our state. There are photographs on my "wish list" that I never got around to taking, and quotes from subjects that Kevin and I never wrote down, but that's the way it goes. This book accounts our individual experiences as we traveled the river, meeting, interviewing and photographing those featured herein, and we hope you enjoy it.

Nearly all the photos were made with Fuji Velvia 50 slide film. I use Nikon equipment, including F4 bodies and focal lengths ranging from 17mm to 420mm. A handful of photos utilize location lighting, and those were assisted by my trusty Lumedyne kit. Jodi and I self-published *The Missouri* using QuarkXPress, Adobe Illustrator and Adobe Photoshop programs on Macintosh computers.

We welcome any and all comments and questions about *The Missouri*, and enjoying hearing about interesting South Dakota subjects. We are planning more books about our great state, and all ideas are appreciated. If you wish to write, please feel free to do so ... I personally guarantee a prompt response. Or, if you want to order any of our books, you can do so online at www.peoplescapes.com. Thanks! Greg

Greg & Jodi Latza / PeopleScapes Inc.
P.O. Box 88821
Sioux Falls, SD 57109
email: glatza@peoplescapes.com

Index

A

Adams Homestead .166
Allen, Garry .108-111
American Creek .107
Apples, Crab .106
Atkinson, Gordy .26-29
Augustine, Donna .71

B

Bad River .73
Bass .144
Baukus, Jim .103
Baumgart, Ray .114
Beach .40, 141
Beautiful Bald Eagle, Sylvan .25
Biegler, Steve .22
Big Bend .96-99
Big Bend Dam .102, 103
Big Foot Ride .16
Big Sioux River .168
Blue Heron .135
Boating .82, 141, 153
Bockholt, Craig .144
Bollig, Herb .142-145
Boots .38
Border, ND & SD .14, 17
Boyer Game Production Area .110
Bridge, Highway 212 .49
Bridge, Meridian .6
Bridge, Railroad .76
Brooks, Grace .71
Buffalo .52-55
Buryanek Rec Area .114
Butterfly, Checkered Skipper .104

C

Cactus, Prickly Pear .57
Cain, David .107
Camping .13, 138
Capitol .74, 75
Cattails .91
Cattle .18, 39, 50, 51, 113
Chalkstone .131
Chamberlain .106-111
Chantier Creek .66
Cheyenne Agency .44, 46
Cheyenne River Tribe .45, 47
Choteau Creek .132
Church .23, 30
Claymore, Michael .47
Cooper, John .78
Cowboys .38, 93

D

Dakota Dunes .167
Dances With Wolves .55
Deer .83
Dogs .39, 55
Doty, Mark .147

E

Eagle, Bald .122
Eagle, Golden .79
Erosion .31
Elk Point .160, 161

F

Farming .56, 105
Farm Island .82, 83
Ferret, Black-Footed .47
Fire .138
Fishing .1, 10, 76, 108-111, 114, 123
Flag .151
Flowers .57, 112, 166
Fog .1
Football .77
Forest City .49
Fort George .91
Fort Pierre .73, 84
Fort Pierre Grassland .90, 92
Fort Manuel .20
Fort Randall .120-128
Fort Sully .57, 82
Fort Thompson .104
Fox, Ajay .33

G

Gallaway Bay .31
Gavins Point .142-147
Gayfeather .104
Geese .86-89, 152
Goat Island .152
Graduation .101
Grassrope, Altwin .96-99
Gries, Ben .161

H

Hands .43, 46, 47
Hartford, Bob & Sara .58-61
Hawk, Northern Harrier .80
Hedren, Paul .152-155
Heisinger, Jim .154-157
Hipple, Bob .64-67
Hofer, Doug .139, 140
Horses .32, 33, 51, 84, 93, 100
Houck Ranch .52-55
Hunhoff, Bernie .7
Hunting .86-89, 116-119, 160
Highway 212 .48, 49

I

Ice .10, 89, 102, 114, 130
Ingle, Kaye .52-55
Iron Nation Recreation Area .95
Irrigation .132

K

Karl Mundt Refuge .122, 123
Kayak .154-157
Keelboat .107
Kenel .20-23, 25
Kirwan, Mike .124-127
Kline Buttes .24
Kruse, Casey .134

L

LaFramboise Island .70-73

La Roche, Dale 100
Lee, Lanniko 16, 42-45
Lightning 68
Lindley Game Production Area 113
Lyman County 9
Lower Brule Sioux 98-101

M

Map 4
Marksville 49
Mau, Melissa 161
Maus, Cy 97
McBride, Ambrose 98
McCowan, Mary Ann 71
Meredith, Rob 94
Missouri River 1-175
Moon 30, 90
Mortenson, Todd 50
Mosasaur 94

N

Narrows 96-99
Nest 149
Niobrara River 133

O

Oahe Dam .64-68
Oak Creek 30, 32, 33
O'Connell, William 23
Olsen, Ole 160

P

Paddlefish 146, 147
Paleontology 94
Parade 39, 151
Paulson, Greg 103
Pebbles 40
Peoria Flats 60, 62, 63
Pheasants .116-119
Pick-Sloan Plan 65, 66
Pickstown 129
Pierre 73-83
Plover, Piping 148
Platte 116-119
Plumegrass 85, 135
Pollock .18, 26-29
Ponca State Park 152-155
Prairie Chickens 92
Pratt, Virginia Jane 128
Press & Dakotan 150
Pries, Roger & Zane 86-89

Q

Qualm Family 116-119
Quartzite 17
Quazi 39

R

Raptors 78-81
Rattlesnakes 34-37
Rieder, Gustav 124-127
Ring 43
Riverboat Days 151
Rocks 40, 46
Rodeo 38
Ronda, James .72
Running Water 135
Russell, Cody 100

S

Sacagawea 20
Sailing 58-61
Sailors, Peggy 71
St. Elizabeth's Mission 30
St. John, Elaine 20
Sand 40
Sandbar 29, 60, 152
Schaefer, Jim .93
Schelske, Norm 133
School 90, 101
Schott Family 34-37
Scott, Greg 110
Seagulls 29
Sedimentation 132-137
Shillingstad, Jack 16, 33, 41
Sioux City 168
Sitting Bull 38, 39, 41
Skunk, Lydia .101
Smith, H.B. 129
Soybeans 132
Spiders 112, 154
Spirit Mound .159
Sports 77, 161
Springfield 133, 136, 137
Standing Rock 24, 49
Storm 115
Sturgeon, Pallid 142-145
Sumac 131, 158
Sunflowers 56

T

Tern, Interior Least 149
Thistle, Russian 63
Three Legs, Bobbi 32
Tiger, Kolt 33
Tipi 71
Trexler-Myren, Virginia 78-81
Tumbleweed .115
Turtle 43
Twillman, Haylee 167

V

Verbana, Woolly 9
Vermillion 154-159

W

Wacipi 25
Wakpala 30, 32, 33
Walleye 108-111
Weinheimer Family 56
Werkmeister, Wayne 153
West Bend Recreation Area 94
Wheat 105
White River 9, 112, 113

Y

Yankton 1, 6, 150, 151

About the Authors

GREG LATZA grew up on a farm near Letcher. He has worked as a newspaper photographer in Kansas, Minnesota and Wisconsin, finally coming home to South Dakota to work at the Sioux Falls *Argus Leader* in 1994. In 1997, Greg and his wife Jodi started PeopleScapes, a freelance photography and graphic design company in Sioux Falls. They have published three other books to date: *Back on the Farm*, *Hometown, S.D.*, and a children's book, *South Dakota: An Alphabetical Scrapbook*. They have two children, Anna and Luke.

KEVIN WOSTER is a native of central South Dakota who grew up fishing and hunting along the Missouri River. He has been a newspaper reporter in this state for more than 25 years, and currently covers western South Dakota and the outdoors for the Sioux Falls *Argus Leader*. He has two grown children, Casey and Meghan, and currently lives in Rapid City with his wife, Mary, and her daughter, Lisa.

For my father, Henry Woster, a farmer and fisherman who believed that touching the water was as important as tending the cows.

— Kevin

Dedicated to Emery Markwed, Jodi's late grandfather. You can see the river from the deck of his Fort Pierre home, and many of the photos in this book were made after spending the night there, my home away from home.

— Greg